Keyboarding

3d Edition

ADAPTED FROM:
Gregg College Keyboarding & Document Processing
7th Edition

Scot Ober, Ph.D.
Professor, Department of Business Education
and Office Administration
Ball State University
Muncie, Indiana

Robert P. Poland, Ph.D.
Professor Emeritus, Business and Distributive Education
Michigan State University
East Lansing, Michigan

Robert N. Hanson, Ed.D.
Professor Emeritus, Department of Office Systems
and Business Education
Northern Michigan University
Marquette, Michigan

Albert D. Rossetti, Ed.D.
Dean, School of Business Administration
Montclair State College
Montclair, New Jersey

Jack E. Johnson, Ph.D.
Professor, Department of Administrative Systems
and Business Education, School of Business
West Georgia College
Carrollton, Georgia

GLENCOE
Macmillan/McGraw-Hill

New York, New York Columbus, Ohio Mission Hills, California Peoria, Illinois

Library of Congress Cataloging-in-Publication Data

Keyboarding: adapted from Gregg college keyboarding & document processing, 7th edition/Scot Ober . . . [et al.].—3rd ed.
p. cm.
Includes index.
ISBN 0-02-801747-1
1. Electronic data processing—Keyboarding. I. Ober, Scot, Date. II. Title: Gregg college keyboarding and document processing for microcomputers basic course.
QA76.9.K48K49 1994 93-8355
652.3—dc20 CIP

Keyboarding, 3d Edition

Imprint 1996

Send all inquiries to:

Glencoe/McGraw-Hill
936 Eastwind Drive
Westerville, OH 43081

ISBN: 0-02-801747-1

Printed in the United States of America.

6 7 8 9 10 11 12 13 14 15 BANT 03 02 01 00 99 98 97 96

Contents

INDEX

Preface

WHAT IS KEYBOARDING?

Keyboarding is the process of inputting or recording data using a keyboard. Operating the keyboard by touch is an essential skill for just about everyone in today's world.

WHO NEEDS KEYBOARDING SKILLS?

The simplest, most accurate answer to this question is that anyone who needs to collect, use, or store information needs keyboarding skills.

Take a look around you. When you make hotel or airline reservations, the reservation clerk uses a keyboard to enter the information. Medical assistants schedule appointments and prepare patient billing records using a keyboard. Most sales people record sales and check stock on hand using a keyboard. Managers and support personnel use a keyboard to collect, manipulate, and store data needed for efficient operations.

In short, keyboarding skill is the key to personal and business productivity. It is an essential communication skill, often required for entering college or qualifying for many types of jobs.

HOW DO YOU LEARN TO KEYBOARD?

The purpose of this book is to enable you to develop effective keyboarding skills in a minimum amount of time. Toward that end, the book is divided into sections.

Reference Section. This 16-page section illustrates standard formats for common business and personal documents including letters, memorandums, reports, tables, forms, and job application correspondence. In addition, the Reference Section includes some basic language arts rules and examples.

Orientation Lesson. This lesson provides an overview of the basic WordPerfect commands needed to complete the first several lessons. Included in this lesson are instructions on how to open WordPerfect, enter commands, move around within a document, and correct errors, as well as instructions on how to save, print, exit, and retrieve a document.

The Alphabet, Number, and Symbol Keys. Lessons 1 through 20 present instructions for learning to operate by touch the alphabetic, number, and symbol keys. The goal at the completion of Lesson 20 is to key 28 words a minute on a 2-minute timed writing with no more than 5 errors.

Ten-Key Numeric Keypad. This section provides instructions for learning to operate by touch the ten-key numeric keypad.

Skillbuilding Activities. Three different types of individualized skillbuilding activities are included that build keyboarding speed and accuracy on both alphabet and number keys. The alphabetic drills may be used at any point after Lesson 9 and the number drills may be used after Lesson 14.

Five-minute timed writings are available if you are required to pass a five-minute timed writing using these basic keyboarding skills for employment.

Like any skill, keyboarding requires practice. By following the carefully developed program instruction in this text, you will develop a communication skill that you can use the rest of your life.

SUPPORTING MATERIAL

The *Keyboarding* software (available in IBM and Macintosh versions) provides individualized instruction that is correlated with each lesson of this textbook. The software program features a completely self-teaching format, flexibility of use, and automatic scoring of all timed writings.

An *Instructor's Manual* for teaching keyboarding is available to all instructors. Included in this manual is an overview of using software to teach keyboarding. Techniques for building straight-copy skill and methods of teaching new keys are also presented.

ACKNOWLEDGEMENTS

We wish to express our appreciation to all the instructors and students who have used the previous editions and who have contributed much to this Third Edition.

The Authors

Reference Section

MICROCOMPUTER SYSTEM

CORRESPONDENCE

REPORTS

EMPLOYMENT DOCUMENTS

TABLES AND FORMS

MISCELLANEOUS

LANGUAGE ARTS

MAJOR PARTS OF A MICROCOMPUTER SYSTEM

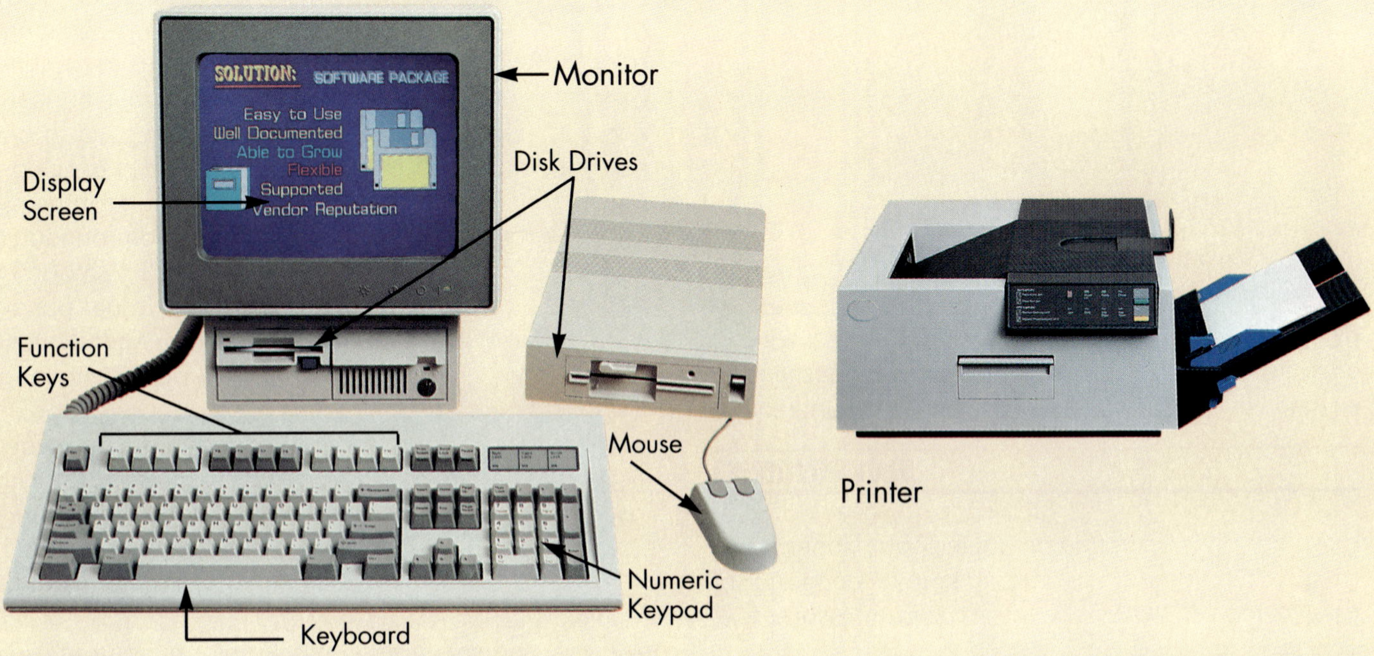

IBM Personal Computer (PS/2)

THE COMPUTER KEYBOARD

AMERICAN HOMES, INC.
One Southeast Financial Center, Miami, FL 33131-3213 Phone: 305-555-7500 • FAX 305-555-7600

↓ 2 inches

September 5, 19-- ↓ 1 inch

Ms. Joan R. Hunter
Bolwater Associates
One Parklands Drive
Darien, CT 06820-3214 ↓ 2

Dear Ms. Hunter ↓ 2

I am returning a signed contract to have your organization conduct a one-day workshop for our employees on eliminating repetitive-motion injuries in the workplace. I understand that this workshop will be applicable for both our office and construction workers.

To enhance the quality and relevance of the workshop, we have made the following changes to the contract:

0.4 inch →
1. We revised Paragraph 4-b to require that the instructor for this workshop be a full-time employee of Bolwater Associates.
2. We added Paragraph 10-c to require our prior approval of the syllabus for the workshop.

If these revisions are satisfactory, please sign and return one copy of the contract for our files. We look forward to this opportunity to enhance the health and well-being of our employees. ↓ 2

Sincerely ↓ 4

John R. Merritt

John R. Merritt, Director
Human Resources Department ↓ 2

jem
Enclosure
c: Legal Department

BUSINESS LETTER IN BLOCK STYLE
(open punctuation)

AMERICAN HOMES, INC.
One Southeast Financial Center, Miami, FL 33131-3213 Phone: 305-555-7500 • FAX 305-555-7600

↓ 2 inches

Center → September 5, 19-- ↓ 1 inch

Ms. Joan R. Hunter
Bolwater Associates
One Parklands Drive
Darien, CT 06820-3214 ↓ 2

Dear Ms. Hunter: ↓ 2

0.5 inch → I am returning a signed contract to have your organization conduct a one-day workshop for our employees on eliminating repetitive-motion injuries in the workplace. I understand that this workshop will be applicable for both our office and construction workers.

To enhance the quality and relevance of the workshop, we have made the following changes to the contract:

0.9 inch →
1. We revised Paragraph 4-b to require that the instructor for this workshop be a full-time employee of Bolwater Associates.
2. We added Paragraph 10-c to require our prior approval of the syllabus for the workshop.

If these revisions are satisfactory, please sign and return one copy of the contract for our files. We look forward to this opportunity to enhance the health and well-being of our employees. ↓ 2

Center →
Sincerely, ↓ 4

John R. Merritt

John R. Merritt, Director
Human Resources Department ↓ 2

jem
Enclosure
c: Legal Department

BUSINESS LETTER IN MODIFIED-BLOCK STYLE
(standard punctuation; indented paragraphs)

AMERICAN HOMES, INC.
One Southeast Financial Center, Miami, FL 33131-3213 Phone: 305-555-7500 • FAX 305-555-7600

↓ 2 inches

September 5, 19-- ↓ 1 inch

Ms. Joan R. Hunter
Bolwater Associates
One Parklands Drive
Darien, CT 06820-3214 ↓ 3

WORKSHOP CONTRACT ↓ 3

I am returning a signed contract to have your organization conduct a one-day workshop for our employees on eliminating repetitive-motion injuries in the workplace. I understand that this workshop will be applicable for both our office and construction workers.

To enhance the quality and relevance of the workshop, we have made the following changes to the contract:

0.4 inch →
1. We revised Paragraph 4-b to require that the instructor for this workshop be a full-time employee of Bolwater Associates.
2. We added Paragraph 10-c to require our prior approval of the syllabus for the workshop.

If these revisions are satisfactory, please sign and return one copy of the contract for our files. We look forward to this opportunity to enhance the health and well-being of our employees. ↓ 5

John R. Merritt

JOHN R. MERRITT, DIRECTOR
HUMAN RESOURCES DEPARTMENT ↓ 2

jem
Enclosure
c: Legal Department

BUSINESS LETTER IN SIMPLIFIED STYLE

↓ 2 inches

Center → January 3, 19-- ↓ 1 inch

Mr. Luis Fernandez, Manager
Customer Relations Department
Arvon Industries, Inc.
1000 Ashland Drive
Russell, KY 41169 ↓ 2

Dear Mr. Fernandez: ↓ 2

As a former employee and present stockholder of Arvon Industries, I wish to protest the planned sale of the Consumer Products Division to Browning Manufacturing Company.

According to published reports, consumer products accounted for 19 percent of last year's corporate profits, and they are expected to account for at least as much this year. In addition, Dun & Bradstreet predicts that consumer products nationwide will outpace the general economy for the next five years.

I am concerned about the effect the planned sale of this division will have on overall corporate profits, on cash dividends for investors, and on the economics of Louisville and Paducah, where the two consumer-products plants are located.

Please ask your board of directors to reconsider this matter. ↓ 2

Center →
Sincerely, ↓ 4

Roger J. Michaelson

Roger J. Michaelson
901 East Benson, Apt. 3
Ft. Lauderdale, FL 33301

PERSONAL-BUSINESS LETTER
(modified-block style; standard punctuation)

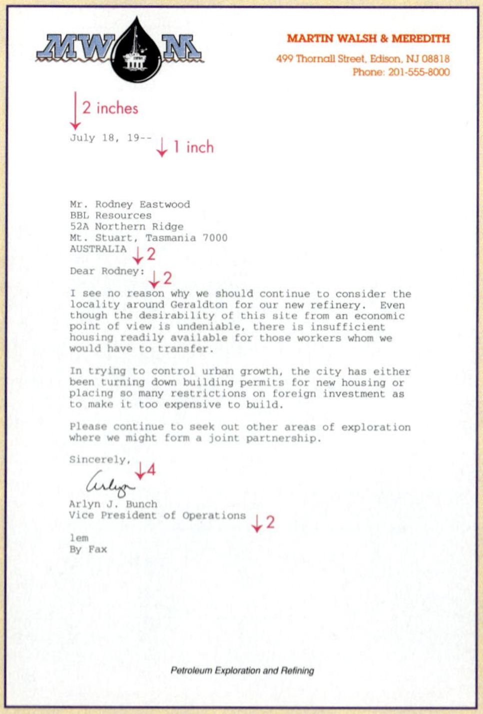

MARTIN WALSH & MEREDITH
499 Thornall Street, Edison, NJ 08818
Phone: 201-555-8000

↓ 2 inches

July 18, 19-- ↓ 1 inch

Mr. Rodney Eastwood
BBL Resources
52A Northern Ridge
Mt. Stuart, Tasmania 7000
AUSTRALIA ↓ 2

Dear Rodney: ↓ 2

I see no reason why we should continue to consider the locality around Geraldton for our new refinery. Even though the desirability of this site from an economic point of view is undeniable, there is insufficient housing readily available for those workers whom we would have to transfer.

In trying to control urban growth, the city has either been turning down building permits for new housing or placing so many restrictions on foreign investment as to make it too expensive to build.

Please continue to seek out other areas of exploration where we might form a joint partnership.

Sincerely, ↓ 4

Arlyn J. Bunch
Vice President of Operations ↓ 2

lem
By Fax

Petroleum Exploration and Refining

BUSINESS LETTER ON MONARCH STATIONERY
(1-inch side margins; $7^1/_4$" × $10^1/_2$")

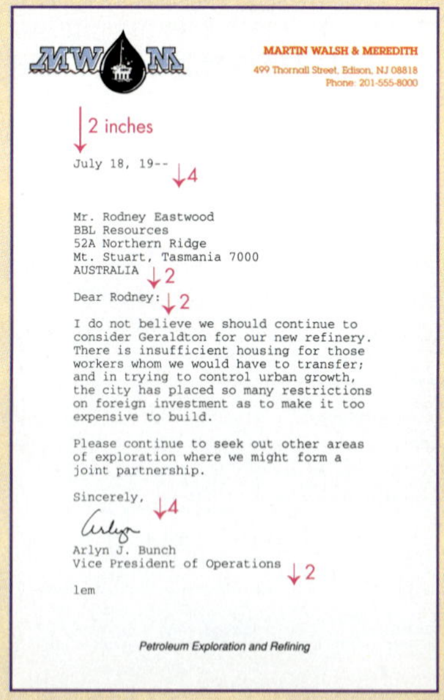

MARTIN WALSH & MEREDITH
499 Thornall Street, Edison, NJ 08818
Phone: 201-555-8000

↓ 2 inches

July 18, 19-- ↓ 4

Mr. Rodney Eastwood
BBL Resources
52A Northern Ridge
Mt. Stuart, Tasmania 7000
AUSTRALIA ↓ 2

Dear Rodney: ↓ 2

I do not believe we should continue to consider Geraldton for our new refinery. There is insufficient housing for those workers whom we would have to transfer; and in trying to control urban growth, the city has placed so many restrictions on foreign investment as to make it too expensive to build.

Please continue to seek out other areas of exploration where we might form a joint partnership.

Sincerely, ↓ 4

Arlyn J. Bunch
Vice President of Operations ↓ 2

lem

Petroleum Exploration and Refining

BUSINESS LETTER ON BARONIAL STATIONERY
(0.75-inch side margins; $5^1/_2$" × $8^1/_2$")

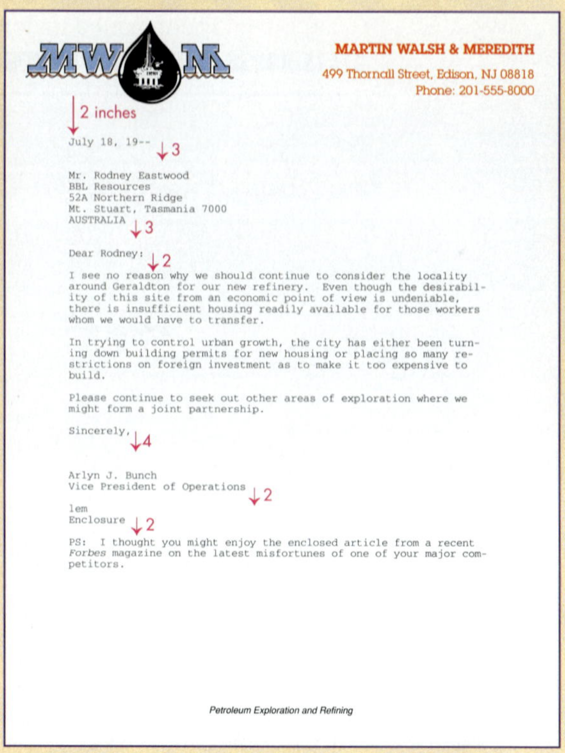

MARTIN WALSH & MEREDITH
499 Thornall Street, Edison, NJ 08818
Phone: 201-555-8000

↓ 2 inches

July 18, 19-- ↓ 3

Mr. Rodney Eastwood
BBL Resources
52A Northern Ridge
Mt. Stuart, Tasmania 7000
AUSTRALIA ↓ 3

Dear Rodney: ↓ 2

I see no reason why we should continue to consider the locality around Geraldton for our new refinery. Even though the desirability of this site from an economic point of view is undeniable, there is insufficient housing readily available for those workers whom we would have to transfer.

In trying to control urban growth, the city has either been turning down building permits for new housing or placing so many restrictions on foreign investment as to make it too expensive to build.

Please continue to seek out other areas of exploration where we might form a joint partnership.

Sincerely, ↓ 4

Arlyn J. Bunch
Vice President of Operations ↓ 2

lem
Enclosure ↓ 2

PS: I thought you might enjoy the enclosed article from a recent *Forbes* magazine on the latest misfortunes of one of your major competitors.

Petroleum Exploration and Refining

BUSINESS LETTER FORMATTED FOR A WINDOW ENVELOPE

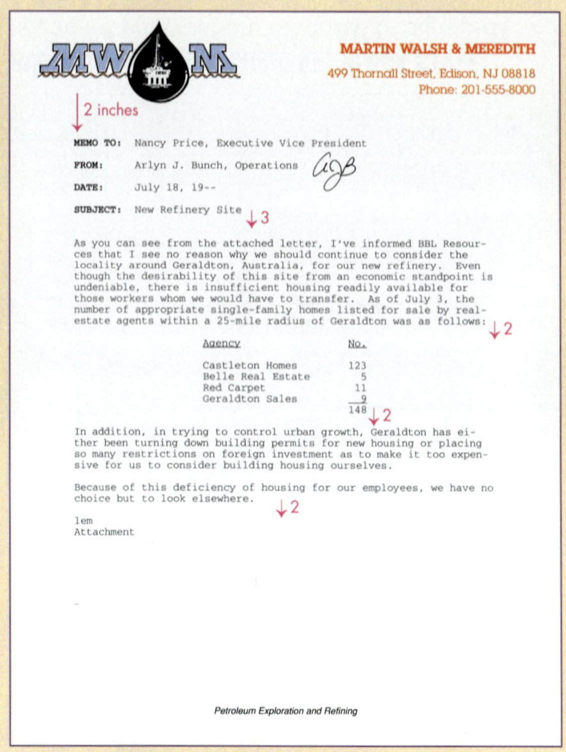

MARTIN WALSH & MEREDITH
499 Thornall Street, Edison, NJ 08818
Phone: 201-555-8000

↓ 2 inches

MEMO TO: Nancy Price, Executive Vice President

FROM: Arlyn J. Bunch, Operations

DATE: July 18, 19--

SUBJECT: New Refinery Site ↓ 3

As you can see from the attached letter, I've informed BBL Resources that I see no reason why we should continue to consider the locality around Geraldton, Australia, for our new refinery. Even though the desirability of this site from an economic standpoint is undeniable, there is insufficient housing readily available for those workers whom we would have to transfer. As of July 3, the number of appropriate single-family homes listed for sale by real-estate agents within a 25-mile radius of Geraldton was as follows: ↓ 2

Agency	No.
Castleton Homes	123
Belle Real Estate	5
Red Carpet	11
Geraldton Sales	9
	148

↓ 2

In addition, in trying to control urban growth, Geraldton has either been turning down building permits for new housing or placing so many restrictions on foreign investment as to make it too expensive for us to consider building housing ourselves.

Because of this deficiency of housing for our employees, we have no choice but to look elsewhere. ↓ 2

lem
Attachment

Petroleum Exploration and Refining

MEMORANDUM

METRO 4 BROADCASTING

200 South Main, Salt Lake City, UT 84101-8675 • Phone: 801-555-3997 • FAX: 801-555-3998

↓ 2 inches

May 5, 19--

↓ 1 inch

Mr. Lester Thompson, Director
British Mutual Broadcasting
24 Portland Place
London W1N 4BB
ENGLAND ↓ 2

Dear Mr. Thompson ↓ 2

Subject: International Study Tour ↓ 2

I have been invited by the Federal Communications Commission to participate in a study of television news programming in European countries. The invitation came from Jill Andrews, FCC vice-chair, and I am, of course, delighted to take part in this project.

As noted on the enclosed report, one function of this study will be to compare the news programming in countries that have a long history of free-access broadcasting with the programming in newly democratic countries. I have been assigned to lead a study group to six European countries to gather first-hand information on this topic. We will be visiting England, France, Germany, Poland, Rumania, and Latvia on August 24 through September 3. In addition to myself, our group will consist of the following members: ↓ 2

Name	Organization	Location
Katherine Grant	WPQR-TV	Los Angeles, CA
Arkady Gromov	National Public Radio	Washington, DC
Manuel Cruz	Miami Herald	Miami, FL
Richard Logan	Cable News System	New York, NY
Barbara Brooks	Federal Comm. Commission	Washington, DC

↓ 2

Our initial plans are to spend at least one full day in each of the countries, meeting with the news programming staff of one or two of the major networks, touring their facilities, viewing recent broadcasts, and, in general, getting a first-hand view of actual news operations and decision-making.

The Voice of Reason for 45 Years

↓ 1 inch

Mr. Lester Thompson
Page 2
May 5, 19-- ↓ 2

Our tentative itinerary calls for us to arrive at Heathrow Airport at 7:10 p.m. on Tuesday evening, August 27. Would it be possible for us to do the following: ↓ 2

1. Meet with various members of your staff on August 28. We would be available from 8:30 a.m. until 1:30 p.m.

0.4 inch →

2. Receive a copy of your programming log for the week of August 26-30 and especially a minute-by-minute listing of the programming segments for your national news reporting. ↓ 2

I would appreciate your contacting Barbara Brooks, our liaison at the Federal Communications Commission (1919 M Street, NW, Washington, DC 20554; phone: 202-555-3894), to let us know whether we may study your operations on August 28.

So that we can finalize our plans and make the necessary arrangements, may we please hear from you by May 15. If your decision is positive, I will work directly with you in coordinating the details of our visit. ↓ 2

Sincerely ↓ 2

METRO BROADCASTING ↓ 4

Denise J. Watterson

Denise J. Watterson
General Manager ↓ 2

urs
Enclosure: FCC Report
By International Express Mail
c: Barbara Brooks ↓ 2

PS: The Federal Communication Commission will reimburse your organization for any expenses associated with our visit, including phone calls, duplicating, and the like.

SPECIAL CORRESPONDENCE FEATURES

FOREIGN ADDRESS. Key the name of a foreign country in all capital letters on a line by itself.

SUBJECT LINE. If used, key a subject line in upper- and lowercase letters below the salutation, with 1 blank line above and below; the terms *Re:* or *In re:* may also be used.

TABLE. Leave 1 blank line above and below a table without a title (regardless of whether the table has column headings) and 3 blank lines above and below a table with a title.

MULTI-PAGE LETTERS. Key the first page on letterhead stationery and the second page on matching plain stationery. On the second page, key the addressee's name, page number, and date beginning 1 inch from the top, blocked at the left margin. Leave 1 blank line between the page-2 heading and the first line of the body.

ENUMERATION. Key the number followed by a period at the point where paragraphs begin (the left margin for blocked paragraphs or indented 0.5 inch for indented paragraphs). Leave 2 spaces after the number and period and indent turnover lines 0.4 inch. Single-space the items within an enumeration and double-space between items.

COMPANY NAME IN CLOSING LINES. If included, key the company name in all capital letters below the complimentary closing, with 1 blank line above and 3 blank lines below it.

REFERENCE INITIALS. Key only the keyboarder's initials (not the signer's) in lowercase letters a double space below the writer's name and/or title. (Optional: You may also include the computer filename; for example: *urs/SMITH.LET*).

ENCLOSURE NOTATION. Key an enclosure notation a single space below the reference initials if an item is enclosed with a letter. Use the term "Attachment" if an item is attached to a memo instead of enclosed in an envelope. Examples: *3 Enclosures, Enclosure: Contract, Attachment.*

DELIVERY NOTATION. Key a delivery notation a single space below the enclosure notation. Examples: *By Certified Mail, By Fax, By Federal Express.*

COPY NOTATION. Key a copy notation *(c:)* a single space below the delivery notation if someone other than the addressee is to receive a copy of the message.

POSTSCRIPT NOTATION. Key a postscript notation as the last item, preceded by 1 blank line. Indent the first line of the postscript if the paragraphs in the body are indented.

FORMATTING ENVELOPES

A standard large (No. 10) envelope is $9^1/_2$ by $4^1/_8$ inches. A standard small (No. $6^3/_4$) envelope is $6^1/_2$ by $3^5/_8$ inches. Although either address format shown below is acceptable, the format shown for the large envelope (all capital letters and no punctuation) is recommended by the U.S. Postal Service for mail that will be sorted by an electronic scanning device.

Window envelopes are often used in a word processing environment because of the difficulty of aligning envelopes correctly in some printers. A window envelope requires no formatting, since the letter is formatted and folded so that the inside address is visible through the window.

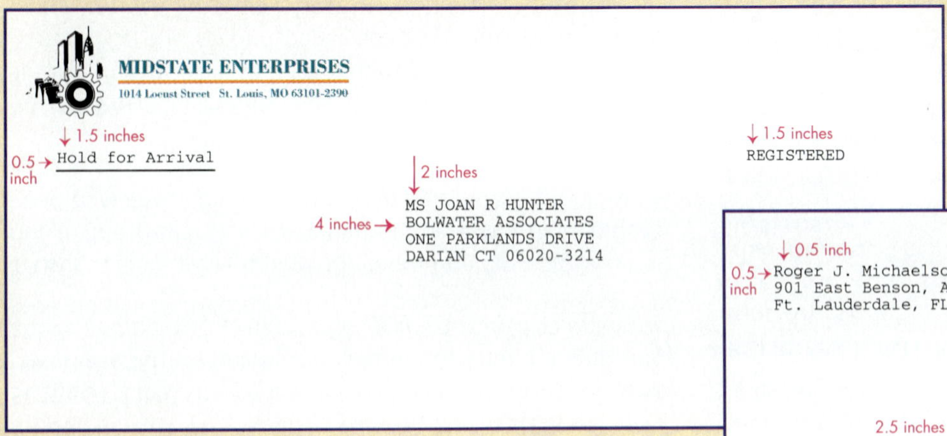

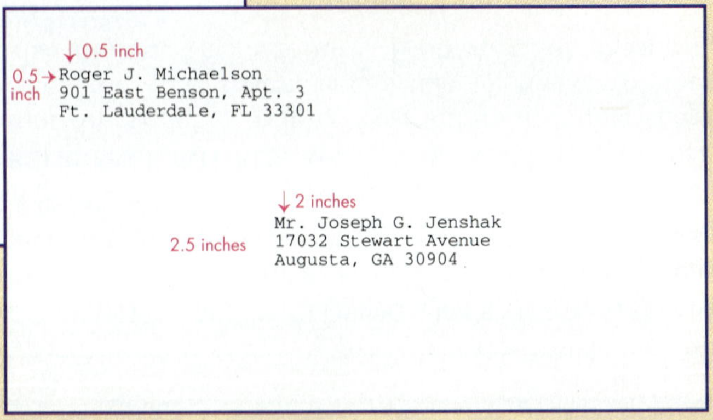

FOLDING LETTERS

To Fold a Letter for a Large Envelope:

1. Place the letter *face up* and fold up the bottom third.
2. Fold the top third down to 0.5 inch from the bottom edge.
3. Insert the last crease into the envelope first, with the flap facing up.

To Fold a Letter for a Small Envelope:

1. Place the letter *face up* and fold up the bottom half to 0.5 inch from the top.
2. Fold the right third over to the left.
3. Fold the left third over to 0.5 inch from the right edge.
4. Insert the last crease into the envelope first, with the flap facing up.

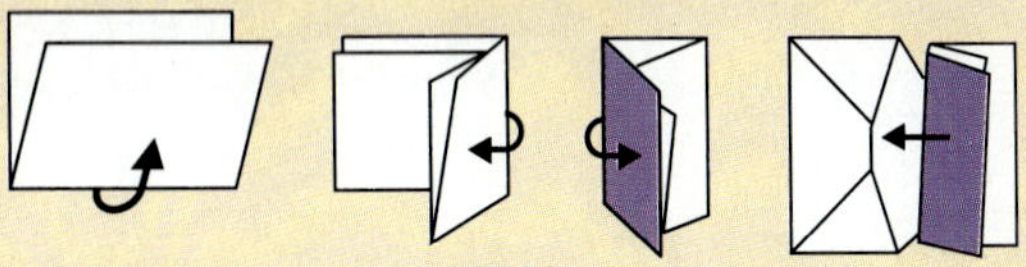

To Fold a Letter for a Window Envelope:

1. Place the letter *face down* with the letterhead at the top and fold the bottom third of the letter up.
2. Fold the top third down so that the address shows.
3. Insert the letter into the envelope so that the address shows through the window.

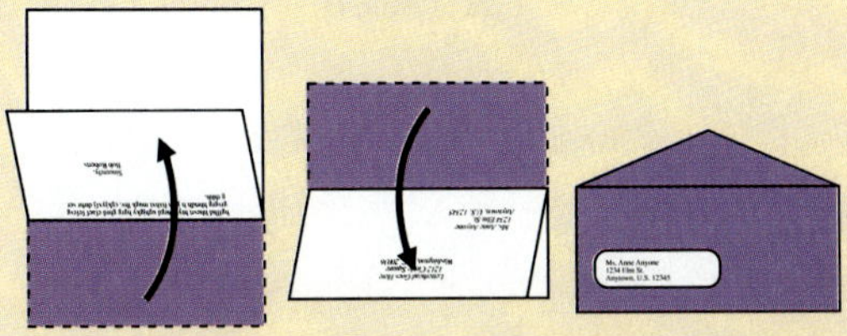

2 inches

THE FEASIBILITY OF IN-HOUSE MANUFACTURING

OF NAIL-POLISH LACQUERS ↓3

I. INTRODUCTION ↓2

0.6 inch → A. Statement of the Problem
B. Scope
C. Procedures
D. Organization of the Report ↓3

II. FINDINGS ↓2

A. Current Manufacturing Processes
1.0 inch → 1. Contract Manufacturing
2. In-House Manufacturing
B. Market Differentiation
1. Image Advertising
2. Product Characteristics
3. Manufacturing Control
C. Advantages and Disadvantages ↓3

III. CONCLUSIONS ↓2

A. Summary of Findings
B. Conclusions and Recommendations

OUTLINE

(Equal top and bottom margins)

CONSOLIDATION OF THE PARTS WAREHOUSES AT ↓2

SIOUX CITY AND CEDAR FALLS ↓2

Maintaining Profitability in a Declining Market ↓15

Prepared by ↓2

Catherine Rogers-Busch
Chief Product Engineer
Helene Ponds and Associates ↓15

December 3, 19--

(Equal top and bottom margins)

TITLE PAGE

2 inches

CONTENTS ↓3

I. DEVELOPMENT ALTERNATIVES	1	↓2
0.6 inch → A. Young Family	2	
B. Growing Family	2	
C. Empty Nest	3	
D. Custom Home	3	↓3
II. FINANCIAL ANALYSES	4	↓2
A. Land-Development Costs	4	
B. Structural Costs	5	
C. Selling Prices	7	↓3
III. RISK ANALYSIS	8	↓2
A. Supply	8	
B. Demand	10	↓3
IV. SUMMARY, CONCLUSIONS, AND RECOMMENDATIONS	14	↓3
APPENDIX ↓2		
A. Questionnaire	17	
B. Lot Plan	19	
C. Cash-Flow Tables	20	↓3
REFERENCES	24	

TABLE OF CONTENTS

2 inches

PREPARING FORMAL REPORTS ↓2

Formatting Guidelines for Writers ↓2

By Keith Stallings ↓3

Formatting formal reports is not a difficult task if you just take the time to study the technical aspects involved. This report discusses report headings, page numbers, margins, reference citations, and the bibliography.

Headings

The major heading in a report is the title. It should be centered in all capital letters 2 inches from the top. A subtitle or byline, if used, is keyed in initial capital letters a double space below the title. The body of the report begins on the third line below the title or byline.

Side Headings. A side heading (such as "Page Numbering" shown below) is keyed at the left margin in initial capital letters and in bold, with double-spacing before and after it.

Paragraph Headings. A paragraph heading is indented and keyed in initial capital letters and in bold a double space below the preceding paragraph. The paragraph heading is followed by a period and two spaces, with the text beginning on the same line.

Page Numbering

The first page of the body of a report is counted as page 1 but is not numbered. All other pages are numbered flush right at the top margin, with the first line of the text beginning a double

UNBOUND REPORT (first page)

↓ 1 inch

2 ↓ 2

a real-estate agent from Central Michigan/Tucker Realty, provided a copy of selected reports that are available only to real estate agents.[1] The relevant statistics for the Mt. Rainey school district for those homes selling for $60,000 or more during the past year are shown in Table 2. ↓ 4

TABLE 2. MT. RAINEY HOME SALES FOR $60,000 OR MORE

Jan-Dec 19--

Selling Price	No. of Homes	Days Listed	Average Sq. Ft.
$60,000-$79,999	55	145	1,571
$80,000-$99,999	29	81	1,917
$100,000-$119,999	7	105	2,094
$120,000-$149,999	8	85	2,291
$150,000 or more	6	109	2,659

↓ 4

The data reflected in Table 2 are based on used homes, so comparisons to newly constructed homes are not always appropriate. According to one source, the typical residential community offers fewer new homes than resales, new homes sell faster, and they average about 20 percent larger than resales.[2] ↓ 2

Young Family ↓ 2

The young family submarket is moving from rental or otherwise limited accommodations into their first new home. The mobile-home ↓ 1

↓ 2

[1]Jacqueline Miller, *Residential Real Estate: Central Michigan Edition*, Michigan Real Estate Association, Lansing, Michigan, 1994, pp. 216-224. ↓ 2

[2]Benjamin J. Ashley, "New Sales Versus Resales: Apples to Oranges?" *Real Estate Quarterly*, September 1993, p.143.

UNBOUND REPORT WITH FOOTNOTES (second page)

↓ 1 inch

13

↓ 2 inches

BIBLIOGRAPHY ↓ 3

0.5 inch →

Ashley, Benjamin J., "New Sales Versus Resales: Apples to Oranges?" *Real Estate Quarterly*, September 1993, pp. 143-149. ↓ 2

Barrett, R. J., "Planning Your First Home," *The Long Island Herald*, September 13, 1992, pp. A3, A16. ↓ 2

Bullard, Mary Helen, *The Bullard Real Estate Report*, Bullard Consulting Group, Nyack, New York, 1994. ↓ 2

Heydenburg, Peter, and Rhonda Silver, "Restrictive Covenants and the Law," *Journal of Real Estate Law*, Vol. 24, No. 3, Fall 1991, pp. 81-87. ↓ 2

Miller, Jacqueline. *Residential Real Estate: Central Michigan Edition*, Michigan Real Estate Association, Lansing, Michigan, 1994.

BIBLIOGRAPHY FOR UNBOUND REPORT

↓ 1 inch

3 ↓ 2

1.5 inches → product was eliminated as an option for this submarket because of the numerous developments of this type that already exist or are under construction in the area.[1]

Modular homes, which have been partially constructed before being brought to the building site, were likewise rejected because: ↓ 2

0.5 inch → Contrary to popular belief, modular homes are generally not less expensive than conventionally constructed homes. Their advantage, instead, is the speed with which they can be constructed. Their major disadvantage relates to the restrictions often placed on them by municipal zoning ordinances.[2] ← 0.5 inch ↓ 2

Since the River Road development is not subject to time pressures, conventional construction methods were evaluated as the most appropriate for this submarket.

Most of the homes sold in Mt. Rainey contain at least three bedrooms, but in the lowest price bracket most contain less than 1,600 square feet, as shown below. ↓ 2

Selling Price	No. of Homes	Days Listed	Average Sq. Ft.
$60,000-$79,999	55	145	1,571
$80,000-$99,999	29	81	1,917
$100,000-$119,999	7	105	2,094
$120,000-$149,999	8	85	2,291
$150,000 or more	6	109	2,659

↓ 2

Because several planning experts have noted the importance of overall outside dimensions for first-time home buyers,[3] the home plan selected for this submarket is only 37 feet wide, allowing it to be placed on a 67-foot-wide lot, with ample setback from the lot lines both from a zoning standpoint and from an aesthetic point of view.

BOUND REPORT WITH ENDNOTES (third page)

↓ 1 inch

13

↓ 2 inches

NOTES ↓ 3

0.5 inch → 1. Jacqueline Miller, *Residential Real Estate: Central Michigan Edition*, Michigan Real Estate Association, Lansing, Michigan, 1994, pp. 216-224. ↓ 2

1.5 inches → 2. Benjamin J. Ashley, "New Sales Versus Resales: Apples to Oranges?" *Real Estate Quarterly*, September 1993, p. 143.

3. Mary Helen Bullard, *The Bullard Real Estate Report*, Bullard Consulting Group, Nyack, New York, 1994, p.3.

4. Peter Heydenburg and Rhonda Silver, "Restrictive Covenants and the Law," *Journal of Real Estate Law*, Vol. 24, No. 3, Fall 1991, pp. 85-87.

5. Bullard, p. 13.

6. R. J. Barrett, "Planning Your First Home," *The Long Island Herald*, September 13, 1992, pp. A3, A16.

7. Heydenburg and Silver, p. 82.

ENDNOTES FOR BOUND REPORT

3

product was eliminated as an option for this submarket because, as Bullard (1994) has noted, numerous developments of this type already exist or are under construction in the area.

Modular homes, which have been partially constructed before being brought to the building site, were likewise rejected for the following reasons (Modlin, 1994, p. 232):

1. Contrary to popular belief, modular homes are generally not less expensive than conventionally constructed homes.
2. Zoning regulations and restrictive covenants often forbid the construction of modular homes, especially in upscale areas.

The big advantage of modular homes is the speed with which they can be constructed. However, since the River Road development is not subject to time pressures, conventional construction methods were evaluated as the most appropriate for this submarket.

Home Requirements. Based on current mortgage criteria in the Mount Rainey area, a buyer in this submarket cannot afford more than $70,000 for a home. Since family size is still small (fewer than four family members), a 1,250-square-foot model with one full bath on each level was selected for planning purposes.

Lot Requirements. Because several planning experts have noted the importance of overall outside dimensions for first-time home buyers (see, for example, Barrett, 1992; Heydenburg and Silver, 1994), the home plan selected for this submarket is only 37 feet wide, which allows it to be located on a 67-foot-wide lot with ample setback from the lot lines.

UNBOUND REPORT WITH AUTHOR/DATE CITATIONS

13

REFERENCES

Connor, E. (1994, June). Body Language Cues. Management Today, pp. 250-261.

LePoole, A. (1988). Your Tour of Duty Overseas (2nd ed.). Oklahoma City: American Press.

LePoole, A. (1990). What American Business Can (and Must) Learn From the Japanese. New York: Management Press.

Newby, C. J. (1994). Global Implications for American Business: The Numbers Don't Lie. Marketing Research Quarterly, 50, 90-215.

Roncaro, P. L. & Lance, G. D. (1992, June 2). Losing Something in the Translation. Winston-Salem Herald, pp. 4A, 12A.

Tell It Like It Is: Making Yourself Understood in the New Russia. (1993, October 19). International Times, p. 38.

REFERENCES PAGE IN APA FORMAT

Jenson 1

Sherlon Jenson

Professor Zhao

Comm 201

8 October 19--

Communication Skills Needed in International Business

International business plays an increasingly important role in the U.S. economy, and U.S. companies recognize that to be competitive nationally, they must be competitive internationally. Reflecting this trend, direct investment by U.S. private enterprises in foreign countries increased from $309 billion in 1987 to $415 billion in 1991, an increase of 34 percent in four years (Connor 253). Today, more than 3,000 U.S. corporations have over 25,000 subsidiaries and affiliates in 125 foreign countries, and more than 25,000 American firms are engaged in international marketing (Newby 193, 205).

International business is highly dependent on communication. According to Arnold LePoole, chief executive officer of Armstrand Industries, an international supplier of automotive parts:

> If a company cannot communicate with its foreign subsidiaries, customers, suppliers, and governments, it cannot achieve success. And the sad fact is that most American managers are ill-equipped to communicate with their international counterparts. (143-144).

Because competent business communication skills are one of the most important components for success in international business affairs, a survey was designed to explore the importance of, level of competence in, and methods of developing four types of

REPORT IN MLA FORMAT

Jenson 13

Works Cited

Connor, Earl. "Body Language Cues." Management Today June 1994: 250-261.

LePoole, Arnold. What American Business Can (and Must) Learn From the Japanese. New York: Management Press, 1990.

---. Your Tour of Duty Overseas. 2nd ed. Oklahoma City: American Press, 1988.

Newby, Corrine J. "Global Implications for American Business: The Numbers Don't Lie." Marketing Research Quarterly 50 (1994): 190-215.

Roncaro, Paul L., and Glenn D. Lance. "Losing Something in the Translation," Winston-Salem Herald 2 June 1992: 4A+.

"Tell It Like It Is: Making Yourself Understood in the New Russia." International Times 19 October 1993: 38.

WORKS-CITED PAGE IN MLA FORMAT

↓ 2 inches

BUCK HARDWARE EXECUTIVE COMMITTEE ↓2

Meeting Agenda ↓2

June 7, 19--, 3 p.m. ↓3

1. Call to order ↓2
2. Approval of minutes of May 5 meeting
3. Progress report on building addition and parking lot (Norman Hedges)
4. Unfinished business:
   a. May 15 draft of Five-Year Plan
   b. Review of National Hardware Association annual convention
5. New business:
   a. Employee grievance filed by Ellen Burrows (John Lennon)
   b. New expense-report forms (Anne Richards)
   c. Home office visit by Jay Nelson
6. Announcements
7. Program: "The One-Second Manager" (30-minute videotape)
8. Adjournment

0.4 → inch

MEETING AGENDA

↓ 2 inches

RESOURCE COMMITTEE ↓2

Minutes of the Meeting ↓2

March 13, 19-- ↓3

ATTENDANCE 1.5 inches → The Resource Committee met on March 13, 19--, at the Airport Sheraton in Portland, Oregon, in conjunction with the western regional meeting. Members present were Michael Davis, Cynthia Giovanni, Don Madsen, and Edna Pintar. Michael Davis, chairperson, called the meeting to order at 2:30 p.m. ↓3

OLD BUSINESS The members of the committee reviewed the sales brochure on electronic copyboards. They agreed to purchase an electronic copyboard for the conference room. Cynthia Giovanni will secure quotations from at least two suppliers.

NEW BUSINESS The committee reviewed a request from the Purchasing Department for three new electronic typewriters. After extensive discussion regarding the appropriate uses of electronic typewriters versus microcomputers, the committee approved the request.

A request from the Marketing Department for a new photocopier was sent back to the department for more justification.

ADJOURNMENT The meeting was adjourned at 4:45 p.m. The next meeting has been scheduled for May 4 in the headquarters conference room. Members are asked to bring with them copies of the latest resource planning document. ↓2

Center → Respectfully submitted, ↓4

D. S. Madsen, Secretary

MINUTES OF MEETING

↓ 2 inches

PORTLAND SALES MEETING ↓2

Itinerary for Arlene Gilsdorf ↓2

March 12-15, 19-- ↓3

Thursday, March 12 ↓2

Detroit/Minneapolis. . . . . Northwest 83
   Leave 5:10 p.m.; arrive 5:55 p.m.
   Seat 8D; nonstop ↓2

0.4 → inch

Minneapolis/Portland . . . . Northwest 2363
   Leave 6:30 p.m.; arrive 8:06 p.m.
   Seat 15C; nonstop; dinner ↓3

Sunday, March 15

Portland/Minneapolis. . . . . Northwest 360
   Leave 7:30 a.m.; arrive 12:26 p.m.
   Seat 15H; one stop; breakfast

Minneapolis/Detroit . . . . Northwest 748
   Leave 1 p.m.; arrive 3:32 p.m.
   Seat 10D; nonstop; snack ↓3

NOTES ↓2

1. Jack Weatherford, assistant western regional manager, will meet your flight on Thursday and return you to the airport on Sunday.
2. All seat assignments are aisle seats; smoking is not allowed on any of the flights.
3. A single-room reservation (Reservation 36812-0), guaranteed for late arrival, has been made at the Airport Sheraton for March 12-14.
4. Important phone numbers:
   Jack Weatherford . . . . .503-555-8029, Ext. 87
   Airport Sheraton 503-555-4032
   Northwest Reservations 800-555-1289

ITINERARY

↓ 2 inches

POWER OF ATTORNEY ↓3

1.0 inch → KNOW ALL MEN BY THESE PRESENTS that I, ANTHONY LEE FERNANDEZ, of the City of Tulia, County of Swisher, State of Texas, do hereby appoint my son, Robert Fernandez, of this City, County, and State as my attorney-in-fact to act in my name, place, and stead as my agent in the management of my real estate transactions, chattel and goods transactions, banking and securities transactions, and business operating transactions.

I give and grant unto my said attorney full power and authority to do and perform all and every act and thing whatsoever requisite and necessary to be done in the said management as fully, to all intents and purposes, as I might or could do if personally present, with full power of revocation, hereby ratifying and confirming all that my said attorney shall lawfully do or shall cause to be done in my behalf by virtue hereof:

IN WITNESS WHEREOF, I have hereunto set my hand and seal this thirteenth day of April, 1994. ↓3

Center → ______________________(L.S.) ↓2

SIGNED and affirmed in the presence of: ↓3

______________________ ↓3

____

Page 1 of 1

↑ 1 inch

LEGAL DOCUMENT

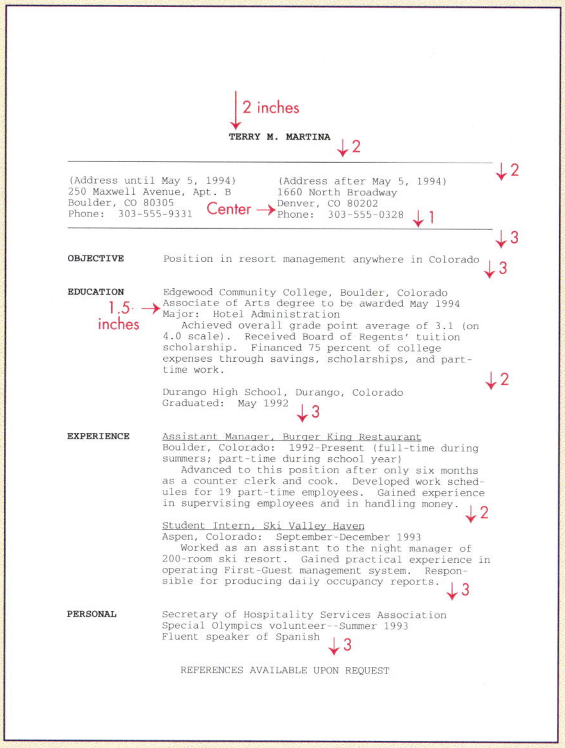

2 inches

TERRY M. MARTINA

(Address until May 5, 1994)
250 Maxwell Avenue, Apt. B
Boulder, CO 80305
Phone: 303-555-9331

(Address after May 5, 1994)
1660 North Broadway
Denver, CO 80202
Phone: 303-555-0328

Center →

OBJECTIVE Position in resort management anywhere in Colorado

EDUCATION Edgewood Community College, Boulder, Colorado
Associate of Arts degree to be awarded May 1994
Major: Hotel Administration
Achieved overall grade point average of 3.1 (on 4.0 scale). Received Board of Regents' tuition scholarship. Financed 75 percent of college expenses through savings, scholarships, and part-time work.

1.5 inches →

Durango High School, Durango, Colorado
Graduated: May 1992

EXPERIENCE Assistant Manager, Burger King Restaurant
Boulder, Colorado: 1992-Present (full-time during summers; part-time during school year)
Advanced to this position after only six months as a counter clerk and cook. Developed work schedules for 19 part-time employees. Gained experience in supervising employees and in handling money.

Student Intern, Ski Valley Haven
Aspen, Colorado: September-December 1993
Worked as an assistant to the night manager of 200-room ski resort. Gained practical experience in operating First-Guest management system. Responsible for producing daily occupancy reports.

PERSONAL Secretary of Hospitality Services Association
Special Olympics volunteer--Summer 1993
Fluent speaker of Spanish

REFERENCES AVAILABLE UPON REQUEST

RESUME

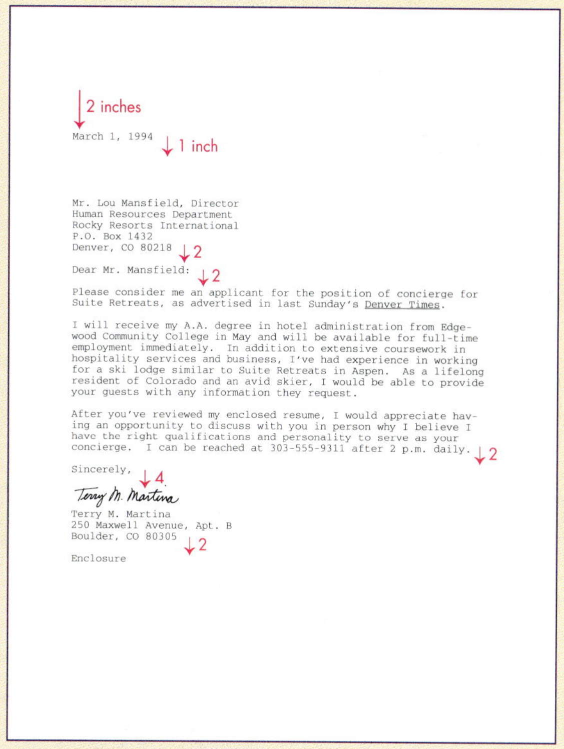

2 inches

March 1, 1994

1 inch

Mr. Lou Mansfield, Director
Human Resources Department
Rocky Resorts International
P.O. Box 1432
Denver, CO 80218

Dear Mr. Mansfield:

Please consider me an applicant for the position of concierge for Suite Retreats, as advertised in last Sunday's Denver Times.

I will receive my A.A. degree in hotel administration from Edgewood Community College in May and will be available for full-time employment immediately. In addition to extensive coursework in hospitality services and business, I've had experience in working for a ski lodge similar to Suite Retreats in Aspen. As a lifelong resident of Colorado and an avid skier, I would be able to provide your guests with any information they request.

After you've reviewed my enclosed resume, I would appreciate having an opportunity to discuss with you in person why I believe I have the right qualifications and personality to serve as your concierge. I can be reached at 303-555-9311 after 2 p.m. daily.

Sincerely,

Terry M. Martina
250 Maxwell Avenue, Apt. B
Boulder, CO 80305

Enclosure

LETTER OF APPLICATION

PLACING INFORMATION ON PRINTED LINES

Because of the difficulty of aligning copy on a printed line with a computer and printer, lined forms such as job-application forms are most efficiently completed on a typewriter.

When keying on a lined form, use the typewriter's variable spacer to adjust the paper so that the line is in the position that a row of underlines would occupy. (On many machines, this is accomplished by pressing in the left platen knob.)

Do not leave any requested information blank; use "N/A" (not applicable) if necessary. Because of space limitations, it may be necessary to abbreviate some words.

Because first impressions are important, ensure that all your employment documents are in correct format, are neat in appearance, and are free from errors.

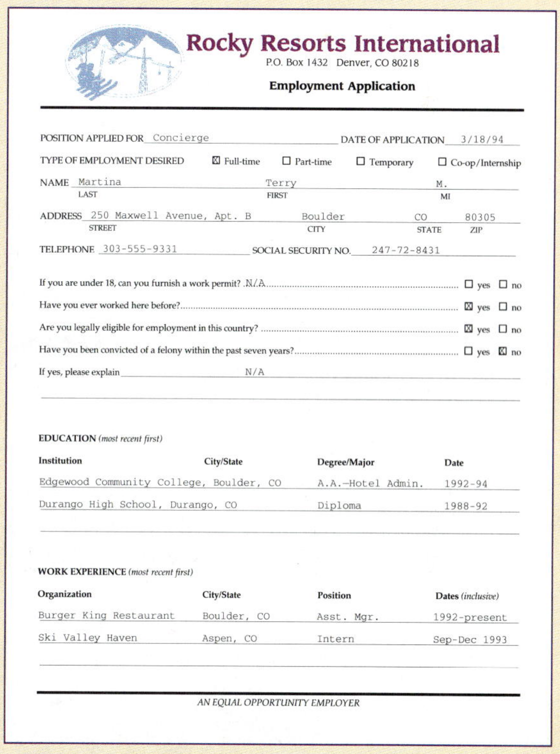

Rocky Resorts International
P.O. Box 1432 Denver, CO 80218
Employment Application

POSITION APPLIED FOR Concierge DATE OF APPLICATION 3/18/94

TYPE OF EMPLOYMENT DESIRED ☒ Full-time ☐ Part-time ☐ Temporary ☐ Co-op/Internship

NAME Martina (LAST) Terry (FIRST) M. (MI)

ADDRESS 250 Maxwell Avenue, Apt. B (STREET) Boulder (CITY) CO (STATE) 80305 (ZIP)

TELEPHONE 303-555-9331 SOCIAL SECURITY NO. 247-72-8431

If you are under 18, can you furnish a work permit? N/A ☐ yes ☐ no

Have you ever worked here before? ☒ yes ☐ no

Are you legally eligible for employment in this country? ☒ yes ☐ no

Have you been convicted of a felony within the past seven years? ☐ yes ☒ no

If yes, please explain N/A

EDUCATION *(most recent first)*

Institution	City/State	Degree/Major	Date
Edgewood Community College,	Boulder, CO	A.A.–Hotel Admin.	1992-94
Durango High School,	Durango, CO	Diploma	1988-92

WORK EXPERIENCE *(most recent first)*

Organization	City/State	Position	Dates *(inclusive)*
Burger King Restaurant	Boulder, CO	Asst. Mgr.	1992-present
Ski Valley Haven	Aspen, CO	Intern	Sep-Dec 1993

AN EQUAL OPPORTUNITY EMPLOYER

JOB-APPLICATION FORM (first page)

ARCHER-DANIELS PHARMACEUTICALS
FRINGE-BENEFIT ANALYSIS

January 1, 19--

Component	Total Costs	Gain
Paid Time Off	$ 5,080	7%
Retirement	3,105	5%
Taxes	2,750	3%
Medical Plan	2,495	107%
Miscellaneous	2,650	14%
TOTALS	$16,080	16%

OPEN TABLE (with blocked column headings)

ARCHER-DANIELS PHARMACEUTICALS
FRINGE-BENEFIT ANALYSIS

January 1, 19--

Component	Costs	Increase
Paid Time Off	$ 5,080	7%
Retirement	3,105	5%
Taxes	2,750	3%
Medical Plan	2,495	107%
Miscellaneous	2,650	14%
TOTALS	$16,080	16%

RULED TABLE (with centered column headings)

Table 14

COMPOUND INTEREST

	Rate of 9%[a]		
Year	Beginning Amount	Interest	Ending Amount
1	$50.00	$ 4.50	$54.50
2	54.50	4.91	59.41
3	59.41	5.35	64.76
4	64.76	5.83	70.59
5	70.59	6.35	76.94
TOTAL	......	$26.94	......

[a]Accrued annually.

BOXED TABLE (with centered column headings)

CHIEF EXECUTIVE ALMA MATERS

As of January 1992

		Education	
Company	Chief Executive	Undergraduate	Graduate
Apple	John Sculley	Brown	Princeton
Compaq	Joseph R. Canion	Houston	Houston
IBM	John F. Akers	Yale	
Unisys	James A. Unruh	Jamestown	Denver
Zenith	Jerry Pearlman	Princeton	Harvard

BOXED TABLE (prepared in WordPerfect)

MASCO SHIPPING LINES

Purchase Order No. 1074

Please ship and bill us for the goods listed below. If for any reason you cannot deliver within 30 days, let us know at once. Please refer to our Purchase Order number in all communications. Your bill to us should indicate all your usual discounts. Payment will be made upon receipt of bill with goods.

To:

Reliable Office Supply
Great Lakes Distribution Center
1001 West Van Buren St.
Chicago, IL 60607

QTY.	CAT. NO.	DESCRIPTION	UNIT PRICE	AMOUNT
120	H02048	Perforated ruled pads	.48	57.60
20	564L04	Correction fluid	1.09	21.80
2	22z398	Paper punch	58.67	117.34
1	B48560	Hi-style tackboard, 24" x 36", burgundy frame/blue fabric	31.98	31.98
20	J22502	Fax rolls	11.33	226.60
500	NS2315	Kraft catalog envelopes, 10" x 13", clasp with gummed flap	104.86	104.86
36	AC7861	Recyclable storage boxes, legal size	3.69	132.84
		Subtotal		693.02
		Shipping and handling (10%)		69.30
		TOTAL AMOUNT DUE		762.32

Date: November 12, 19-- _______________ Purchasing Agent

BUSINESS FORM

FORMATTING BUSINESS FORMS

Most business forms can be formatted most efficiently on a typewriter. Whether formatted on a typewriter or computer, follow these guidelines:

- Align number columns at the right, centered visually within each ruled area.
- Align word columns (or combination word and number columns) at the left, 2 or 3 spaces after the vertical rule.
- Set the left margin for the first column and set left or decimal tabs for each additional column.
- Do not key a dollar sign for amount columns.
- Indent turnover lines 2 or 3 spaces.

WORD-DIVISION RULES

1. Do not divide words pronounced as one syllable *(thoughts, planned)*, contractions *(shouldn't, haven't)*, or abbreviations *(UNICEF, assoc.)*.
2. Divide words only between syllables. Whenever you are unsure of where a syllable ends, consult a dictionary.
3. Leave at least three characters (the last will be a hyphen) on the upper line, and carry at least three characters (the last may be a punctuation mark) to the next line. Thus *de- lay* and *af- ter*, but not *a- maze* or *trick- y*.
4. Divide compound words either at the hyphen *(self-confidence)* or where the two words join to make a solid compound. Thus *master- piece*, not *mas- terpiece*.

PROOFREADERS' MARKS

Proofreaders' Mark	Draft	Final Copy
SS Single-space	SS [first line second line	first line second line
ds Double-space	ds [first line second line	first line second line
V or ∧ Insert punctuation	if hes not	if he's not,
new / ~~old~~ Change word	and ~~if~~ you (when)	and when you
Delete and close up	co/operation	cooperation
/ Use lowercase letter	our President	our president
○ Spell out	the only (1)	the only one
] Move right	Please send	Please send
[Move left	May I	May I

Proofreaders' Mark	Draft	Final Copy
⁀ Omit space	data base	database
∽ Transpose	they all see	they see all
∧ Insert	she may go (not)	she may not go
≡ Capitalize	Maple street	Maple Street
Delete	a ~~final~~ draft	a draft copy
Move as shown	no (copy) machine	no machine
¶ Paragraph	¶ Most of the	Most of the
# Insert space	allready to	all ready to
⊙ Make a period	one way	one way.
... Don't delete	a ~~true~~ story	a true story

PUNCTUATION AND SPACING POINTERS

AMPERSAND. One space before and after.

CLOSING QUOTATION MARK. *(a)* Keyed *after* a period or comma and *before* a colon or semicolon. *Always. (b)* Keyed *after* a question mark or exclamation point if the quoted material is a question or an exclamation; otherwise, it is keyed *before* the question mark or exclamation point.

COLON. Two spaces after.

COMMA. One space after.

EQUALS SIGN. One space before and after.

EXCLAMATION POINT. Two spaces after.

PERIOD. *(a)* Two spaces after a period at the end of a sentence; *(b)* one space after the period following someone's initials or the abbreviation of a single word (e.g., *Mrs. Jones*); *(c)* no space after each internal period in an abbreviation (e.g., *a.m.*).

QUESTION MARK. Two spaces after.

SEMICOLON. One space after.

TABLE COLUMNS. Six spaces between.

UNDERLINE. *(a)* To key a magazine or book title, underline the entire title, including internal spaces and punctuation. *(b)* To stress individual words, underline them separately; do not underline the punctuation or the spaces between the words.

ZIP CODE. One space before.

COMMAS

1. Use a comma to separate two independent clauses in a compound sentence when they are joined by *and, but, or,* or *nor.*

   I want to attend, but Dee has tickets to the game.

   Ellen left her job in May, and she and her sister went to Paris.

   But: Ellen left her job and went to Paris with her sister.

2. Use commas to separate three or more items in a series when the last item is preceded by *and, or,* or *nor.*

   Patsy, Kris, or Bill will be elected.

   They saved their work, exited the program, and turned their computers off.

3. When a dependent clause *precedes* the independent clause, separate the clauses with a comma.

   Before we can make a decision, we need the facts.

4. Use commas to set off a nonessential expression (a word, phrase, or clause that may be omitted without changing the basic meaning of the sentence). When an expression is essential to the completeness of a sentence, do not set it off with commas.

   Our present projections, you must admit, are inadequate.

   But: You must admit the projections are inadequate.

   It was mailed on Tuesday, the day your order was received.

   But: It was mailed the day your order was received.

5. Use commas to set off the year when it follows the month and day.

   The reunion will be held on May 2, 1995, in Chicago.

   But: The reunion will be held on May 2 in Chicago.

   But: In March 1988 the firm was incorporated.

6. When two adjectives modify the same noun, use a comma to separate the adjectives if they are not joined by *and.* (Note: If the first adjective modifies the combined idea of the second adjective plus the noun, do not separate the adjectives with a comma.)

   Rue is an intelligent, understanding counselor.

   But: Rue is an intelligent and understanding counselor.

7. Use commas to set off a transitional expression (such as *therefore*) or an independent comment (such as *of course*).

   Thomas told her, however, that the new printers would arrive today.

   In the first place, the members have not yet reached an agreement.

8. Use commas to set off an expression in apposition (that is, a word, phrase, or clause, that identifies or explains other terms).

   The projectionist, Kelsey Auland, will show the film tonight.

OTHER PUNCTUATION MARKS

1. Use a semicolon to separate two independent clauses that are not joined by *and, but,* or *nor.*

   Leslie worked on Labor Day; Jean did not.

   But: Leslie worked on Labor Day but Jean did not.

2. If either of the independent clauses in a compound sentence contains a comma, separate the clauses with a semicolon rather than a comma.

3. Use a semicolon to separate items in a series if any of the items already contain commas.

   Staff meetings were held on Thursday, May 7; Monday, June 7; and Friday, June 12.

4. Hyphenate a compound adjective (two or more words that function as a unit to describe a noun) that comes *before* a noun. Exception: If the first word is an adverb ending in *ly,* do not hyphenate such adjectives.

   The determination of production goals for each of the plants is a high-level decision.

   But: Decisions about production goals are made at a high level.

5. Underline titles of complete published works, and use the quotation marks around titles that represent only a part of a complete published work.

   The chapter entitled "IRAs and Personal Financial Planning" will be discussed tomorrow.

   The sales director reported that excellent results had been obtained from advertisements in the Chicago Tribune.

6. Use a period to end a sentence that is a polite request, suggestion, or command if you expect the reader to respond by acting rather than by giving a yes-or-no answer.

   Will you please send the report by overnight express.

   May I have a copy of your report before you leave.

7. To make a singular noun possessive, add the apostrophe before the *s.*

   a customer's request the company's profits

8. To make a possessive from a singular noun that ends in an *s* sound, be guided by the way the word is pronounced. If a new syllable is formed by making the noun possessive, add an apostrophe and an s (my *boss's* office, the *witness's* testimony). If the addition of an extra syllable to a singular noun would make a word that is hard to pronounce, add only an apostrophe (*Mr. Phillips'* career, *Mrs. Hodges'* friend).

9. To make a plural noun not ending in s possessive, place the apostrophe before the s.

   the women's offices the children's school

10. To make a possessive from a plural noun ending in *s,* place the apostrophe after the *s.*

    the secretaries' computers the Halls' reception

11. Do not use an apostrophe with possessive pronouns.

    The new house is ours. The team won its first three debates.

    But: It's time for their mid-semester exams.

CAPITALIZATION

1. Capitalize the first word of all sentences and the first word of expressions used as a sentence.
   How may I help you?
   Enough said about that!

2. Capitalize every proper noun. A proper noun is the official name of a particular person, place, or thing.
   Ohio State University Memorial Day

3. Capitalize common organization terms such as *advertising department* and *finance committee* when they are the actual names of units within the writer's own organization and are modified by the word *the.*
   The Board of Trustees of our college meets on Thursday.
   The advertising department of A & G will reorganize.

4. Capitalize adjectives derived from proper nouns.
   America (n.) American (adj.)

5. Capitalize the names of places such as *streets, buildings, parks, monuments, rivers, oceans,* and *mountains.* Do not capitalize short forms used in place of the full name.
   Northland Mall Front Street
   Pacific Ocean Washington Monument

6. Capitalize *north, south, east, west,* and derivative words when they designate definite regions or are an integral part of a proper name.
   She lives in the Southwest.
   Go north for two blocks, then head west.
   He is a southern gentleman.

7. Capitalize the names of the days of the week, months, holidays, and religious days.
   Veterans Day Tuesday, October 8

8. Do not capitalize the names of the seasons.
   We will publish the book in the fall.
   During the spring, my allergies bother me.

9. Capitalize the names of specific course titles. Do not, however, capitalize the names of subjects or areas of study (except for any proper nouns or adjectives in such names).
   I'm enrolled in American History 201.
   She's studying modern art.

10. Capitalize a noun followed by a number or letter that indicates sequence. Exceptions: Do not capitalize the nouns *line, note, page, paragraph, size.*
    The Section 2 class was assigned Chapter 5.
    Many read only pages 15–27.

NUMBERS

1. Spell out numbers 1 though 10, and use figures for numbers above 10. Exception: If two or more *related* numbers both below and above 10 are used in the same sentence, use figures for all numbers.
   She invited seven managers to the meeting.
   There were 20 people at the seminar.

2. To express even millions or billions, use the following style: 35 million; 7 billion.
   20 million (**not** 20,000,000)
   $45 billion (**not** 45,000,000,000)

3. When two numbers come together in a sentence and one is part of a compound adjective, spell out the first number unless the second number would make a much shorter word.
   three 9-room suites 175 six-page reports

4. When expressing numbers in words, hyphenate all compound numbers between 21 and 99 (or *21st* and *99th*), whether they stand alone or are part of a number over 100.
   They sent forty-six invitations.

5. Spell out (and hyphenate) fractions that stand alone, and use figures for mixed numbers.
   four-fifths of the market $7\,{}^{3}/_{8}$ yards

6. To form the plural of figures, add *s* (without the apostrophe).
   the 1990s

7. Spell out a number at the beginning of a sentence.
   Seven students missed the class.

8. Use commas to separate thousands, millions, and billions.
   $12,752,099 10,000 199,999

9. Use figures for house numbers.
   They live at 10 Eastland Drive.

10. Do not use a decimal with even amounts of money.
    $550 (**Not:** $550.00)

11. Use the word *cents* for amounts under $1.
    75 cents (**Not:** $.75 or 75¢)

12. Use *st, d,* or *th* only if the day precedes the month.
    Start the work on the 3rd of June.
    But: Start work on June 1.

13. Use figures to express time with *o'clock* or with *a.m.* and *p.m.* (The abbreviations *a.m.* and *p.m.* should be keyed in small letters without spaces.)
    9 o'clock (**Not:** nine o'clock)
    I left at 8:30 a.m. and returned at 5 p.m.

14. Express percentages in figures and spell out the word *percent.* Note: The percent sign (%) may be used in tables.
    7 percent 15.6 percent

15. When ages are used as significant statistics, express them in figures. Otherwise, spell them out.
    You may drive at the age of 16.
    My father is seventy-five years old.

ABBREVIATIONS

1. In lowercase abbreviations made up of single initials, use a period after each initial but no space after each internal period.
   p.m. i.e. f.o.b.

2. Always abbreviate *Mr., Mrs., Ms.,* and *Dr.,* when they are used with personal names. In general, spell out all other titles used with personal names.
   Ms. Joan Brandt Dr. James Rich

3. Always abbreviate *Jr., Sr.,* and *Esq.* when they follow personal names.
   Mr. Harold A. Smith, Jr. George Barr, Esq.

4. Spell out compass points used as ordinary nouns and adjectives or when included in street names. Exception: Abbreviate compass points without periods when they are used *following* a street name.
   He bought a lot on the southeast corner.
   18 Front Street, NW
   12 North Adams Street

5. In nontechnical writing, spell out units of measure.
   a 5-quart bottle 12 yards of material
   $3^1/_2$ by 5 inches a 110-acre development

6. Abbreviate units of measure when they occur frequently, as in technical or scientific works, on forms, and in tables. Do not use periods.
   14 oz 6 qts 5 ft 10 in 55 mph

GRAMMAR

1. A verb must agree with its subject in number and person.
   They are looking for the dog.
   He is looking for them.

2. The following pronouns are always singular and take singular verbs: *each, either, neither, much,* and pronouns ending in *body, thing,* and *one.*
   Neither of the assistants is busy.
   Everybody has to participate.

3. When establishing agreement between subject and verb, disregard intervening phrases and clauses.
   The doctor, not the interns, is working there.
   Only one of the students finished the test.

4. Verbs in the subjunctive mood (those that talk of conditions which are improbable, doubtful, or contrary to fact) require the plural form.
   I wish I were on that harbor cruise.
   If I were she, I would use a different format.

5. Use a singular pronoun with a singular antecedent (the word for which the pronoun stands) and a plural pronoun with a plural antecedent.
   Neither Karla nor Marie must change her coat.
   Neither Mr. Brown nor his aides finished their work.

6. Use nominative pronouns (*I, he, she, we, they,* and so on) as subjects of a sentence or clause.
   The programmer and he are reviewing that.
   It is she who likes this software program.

7. Use objective pronouns (*me, him, her, us, them,* and so on) as objects in a sentence or clause.
   The folders are for Susan and him.
   She went out with him and me.

8. Use comparative adjectives and adverbs (*er, more,* and *less*) in referring to two persons, places, or things; use superlative adjectives and adverbs (*est, most,* and *least*) in referring to more than two.
   He is the quicker of the two ball players.
   He is the quickest of the two ball players.
   This computer is faster than the other.
   This computer is the fastest of all.

Orientation Lesson

This orientation lesson provides an overview of the basic WordPerfect commands you will need to use in the first several lessons. Study these commands; then return to this lesson for review as you progress through the first several lessons.

A. OPENING WORDPERFECT

DOS prompt > WP

Example:
C:*WP*

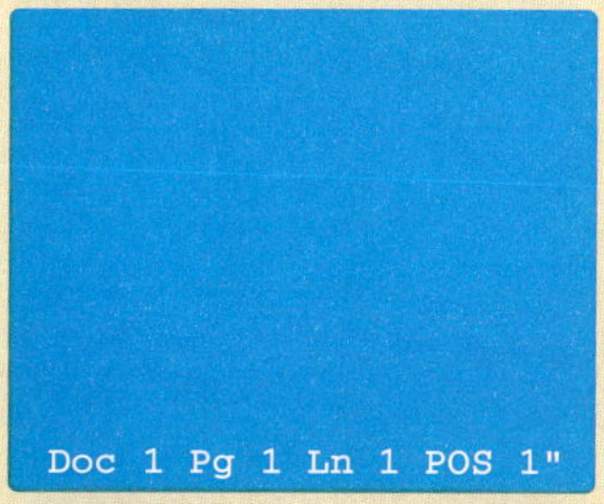

Follow the directions for your computer system for turning on your computer and beginning WordPerfect (usually you would key "WP" at the DOS prompt).

WordPerfect opens with a blank screen. The *cursor* (a blinking underline at the top left of the screen) indicates your current position. The *status line* at the bottom right of the screen shows the cursor position. When you begin, the status line will show that the cursor is positioned in Document 1, Page 1, Line 1″ (vertical position in inches from the top of the page), and Position 1″ (horizontal position in inches from the left edge of the page).

To enter text, you begin keying. Text will be inserted at the cursor position. When the cursor reaches the end of a line, it will automatically move to the beginning of the next line. This feature, called *word wrap,* means you press Enter only to begin a new line or a new paragraph.

B. ENTERING COMMANDS

Display menu bar: Alt-=
Remove menu bar: Esc or Alt-=

Exit (execute a command): F7

Cancel: F1

Help: F3

WordPerfect features may be selected by pressing a function key—either alone or in combination with the Alt (Alternate), Ctrl (Control), or Shift keys.

WordPerfect 5.1 also offers pull-down menus. To turn on pull-down menus, hold down the Alt key while pressing the equal (=) key. To select a function from the pull-down menu, either key the highlighted letter of the function you want or use the arrow keys or a mouse to highlight the selection.

Although using pull-down menus may be helpful for the new or occasional user, using function keys requires fewer keystrokes. For this reason, the WordPerfect commands in this text are given only for function keys.

With the use of function keys or pull-down menus, many commands require you to press F7 to exit (or execute) a command. To cancel a command, you would press F1.

If you need help, press F3 once to display the help screen and twice to display a keyboard template showing the keystrokes for the most common commands.

C. MOVING AROUND WITHIN A DOCUMENT

In the commands that follow, a hyphen joins keys that must be held down together; a comma separates keys that are pressed one after the other. For example, the command "Sh-F7, 1" means to *(a)* hold down the shift key, and while still holding it down, *(b)* press the F7 key; *(c)* release the shift and F7 keys; and *(d)* key *1*.

To move the cursor around within a document, you can use either the arrow (cursor movement) keys or a mouse to reposition the cursor. The arrow keys are located at the bottom right of most keyboards. When used alone or with other function keys, they enable you to quickly move to any position within your document. Use the commands shown at the right to move the cursor to the positions indicated.

Movement	Keys
Word left	Ctrl-←
Word right	Ctrl-→
Beginning of line	Home, ←
End of line	Home, → (*or* End)
Top of screen	Home, ↑
Bottom of screen	Home, ↓
Previous page	PgUp
Next page	PgDn
Beginning of document	Home, Home, ↑
End of document	Home, Home, ↓

D. CORRECTING ERRORS

To insert new text into your document, position the cursor where you want to add the text and begin keying. Text to the right of the cursor will move to the right to make room for the new text. Use the commands shown at the right to delete unwanted text.

Delete	Keys
Character at cursor	Delete
Character to the left of cursor	Backspace
Word at cursor	Ctrl-Backspace
From cursor to end of line	Ctrl-End
Undelete (restore deleted text)	F1, 1

E. PRINTING A DOCUMENT

WP

Print:
Document: Sh-F7, 1
Page: Sh-F7, 2

Once a printer has been selected during the installation of WordPerfect, the print feature enables you to print all or part of a document on screen or a document that has previously been saved. To print an entire document that is on screen, press Sh-F7 (Print) and enter "1" (Full Document). To print a single page, position the cursor on the page you want to print, then press Sh-F7 (Print) and "2" (Page). To print multiple pages of a single document, press Sh-F7 and enter "5." Next, enter the page numbers of those pages that you want to print (for example, 3–6).

F. SAVING A DOCUMENT

WP

Save:
First time: F10, *file name,* Enter
Thereafter: F10, Enter, *Y*

To avoid accidental loss of data, you should save your work frequently. To save a document periodically while you are working on it, press F10 (Save). The first time you save a document, you must give it a file name, such as "MEMO-3." The file name can be up to 8 characters with no spaces. Once you have named the file, pressing F10 will give you a choice of replacing the earlier version of the document with the new version (the usual choice) or saving the new version under a different name.

G. EXITING A DOCUMENT AND WORDPERFECT

WP

Exit: F7

To exit a document you are working on, press F7 (Exit). You will be asked if you want to save your work. Enter "Y" if you wish to do so. If you are saving the document for the first time, you will be asked to give the document a name. If the document has already been named, you will be asked if you want to replace it with the new version. Then you will be asked if you want to exit WordPerfect. Enter "Y" to exit the program and return to a DOS prompt or "N" to clear the screen and start a new document. If you choose to exit WordPerfect, do not remove your disk from the drive until you see a DOS prompt on the screen.

File name known:
Sh-F10, *file name,* Enter
File name unknown (List Files):
F5, Enter, *highlight file name,* 1

H. RETRIEVING A FILE

To work on a previously saved file (document), first start WordPerfect as usual. Then to retrieve the file, press Sh-F10 (Retrieve), enter the name of the file you want, and press Enter. If you cannot remember the name of the file, press F5 (List Files) and Enter. Use the arrow keys to highlight the name of the file you want to retrieve, then enter "1."

Delete file:
F5, *highlight file name, 2, Y*

I. DELETING A FILE

When you are sure you no longer need a file that has been saved on disk, you should delete it. Keep in mind that once you delete a file, you can never retrieve it. To delete a file, press F5 (List) to list the file names, then use the arrow keys to highlight the file you want to delete. Enter "2" (Delete) and "Y" (Yes).

```
12-point monospaced font
10-point monospaced font
```

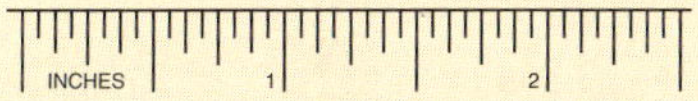

LINE SPACING

```
single  1.5  double  triple
single
         1.5
single       double
single  1.5          triple
```

J. LEARNING ABOUT FONTS AND LINE SPACING

Fonts (different styles and sizes of type) are available through your printer or through WordPerfect. Dot-matrix printers usually have fonts of 10 cpi (characters per inch) and 12 cpi. Laser printers and some of the more sophisticated dot-matrix printers also have fonts available in different point sizes (measured by the height of the letters), different typefaces (style of characters), and proportional spacing.

The jobs in this text have been planned for using 10 cpi, a monospaced font where each character of space in a line takes the same amount of space. This is the default for most dot-matrix printers.

The default line spacing for WordPerfect is 1 (single spacing) which leaves no blank lines between keyed lines. Line spacing can be changed to any number, including fractions. Line spacing of 1.5 leaves a half line between keyed lines; 2 leaves 1 blank line; 3 leaves 2 blank lines, and so on.

K. LEARNING ABOUT MARGINS

Margins are the white (empty) space around all sides of a printed document. The default top, bottom, and side margins for a standard sheet of paper (8 1/2" × 11") are 1 inch. No matter what size font you use, the margins will not change.

When you begin a new document in WordPerfect, the status line indicates that your cursor is on Ln 1" (top margin) and Pos 1" (left margin). Even though no margins show on the screen, the printed page will have 1-inch margins.

In order for your printer to print with the appropriate margins, you must insert the paper correctly into the printer. Learn how to operate the printer you will be using so that your documents will print with the correct margins.

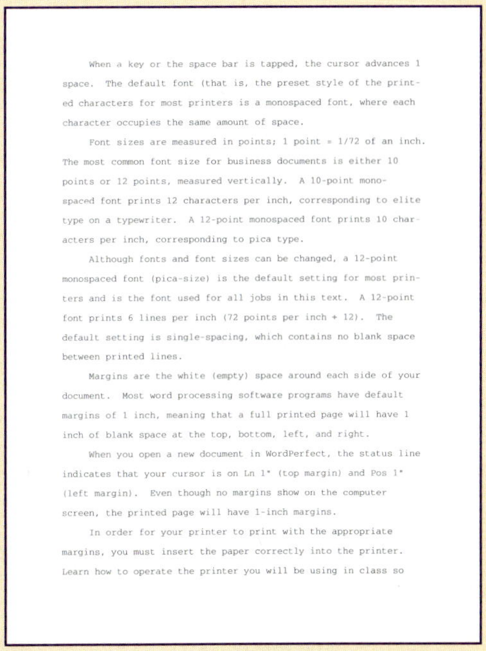

When a key or the space bar is tapped, the cursor advances 1 space. The default font (that is, the preset style of the printed characters for most printers is a monospaced font, where each character occupies the same amount of space.

Font sizes are measured in points; 1 point = 1/72 of an inch. The most common font size for business documents is either 10 points or 12 points, measured vertically. A 10-point monospaced font prints 12 characters per inch, corresponding to elite type on a typewriter. A 12-point monospaced font prints 10 characters per inch, corresponding to pica type.

Although fonts and font sizes can be changed, a 12-point monospaced font (pica-size) is the default setting for most printers and is the font used for all jobs in this text. A 12-point font prints 6 lines per inch (72 points per inch ÷ 12). The default setting is single-spacing, which contains no blank space between printed lines.

Margins are the white (empty) space around each side of your document. Most word processing software programs have default margins of 1 inch, meaning that a full printed page will have 1 inch of blank space at the top, bottom, left, and right.

When you open a new document in WordPerfect, the status line indicates that your cursor is on Ln 1" (top margin) and Pos 1" (left margin). Even though no margins show on the computer screen, the printed page will have 1-inch margins.

In order for your printer to print with the appropriate margins, you must insert the paper correctly into the printer. Learn how to operate the printer you will be using in class so

L. PRACTICING BASIC WORDPERFECT COMMANDS

1. To begin WordPerfect, you will need to be in the WordPerfect directory. At the DOS prompt (C:>), key CD\WP51. At the WordPerfect prompt (C:\WP51>), key WP to start the program (or use the correct procedure for your system).
2. Files created in WordPerfect are called data files. Data files can be saved on a disk in a drive other than the default drive (the drive letter showing when you turn on your computer). To save a file, you must enter the path (drive where it is to be saved) and the name of the document.
3. To move the cursor around in a document, use the cursor movement commands shown in Section C, page OL-2.
4. If you were working on the document shown in Illustration 1, when you retrieved the document, your cursor would be positioned under the "T" in "To," with Ln 1" Pos 1" showing on the status line at the bottom right of the screen.
5. If you press tab, the first line of the paragraph will be indented 0.5 inch (the default tab).

   Note in Illustration 2 that when the tab key is pressed, the last words on the first line moved (wrapped around) to the second line.
6. To delete a word and the space after it, position the cursor any place within that word and press Ctrl-Backspace. Note that when a word is deleted (such as *automatically* in the fourth line), the space around the word is closed up.
7. To save a document on a separate data disk, press F10. When asked for the document name, key the complete path name for the file (for example, A:\PRACTICE).
8. To print a document, press Sh-F7, 1.
9. To exit a document and return to a new document screen, press F7. If you have not saved the file before now, or if you have made any changes to the file, answer *yes* to save; then enter the path name.
10. To exit a document and WordPerfect, press F7. Answer *yes* or *no* to save the document, and answer *yes* to exit WordPerfect.
11. When you see the DOS prompt and that the disk drive light is off, you may safely remove your data disk.

ILLUSTRATION 1

```
To enter text, simply begin keying.  The text will be inserted at
the current cursor location.  Errors can be corrected easily by
simply backspacing and keying the correct letter.  When the
cursor reaches the end of a line, it will automatically move to
the next line.  This feature, called word wrap, means you do not
have to press Enter unless you wish to begin a new paragraph or a
new drill line.  Many other features of WordPerfect make creating
business documents fast and simple.
```

ILLUSTRATION 2

```
     To enter text, simply begin keying.  The text will be
inserted at the current cursor location.  Errors can be corrected
easily by simply backspacing and keying the correct letter.  When
the cursor reaches the end of a line, it will move to the next
line.
     This feature, called word wrap, means you do not have to
press Enter unless you wish to begin a new paragraph or a new
drill line.  Many other features of WordPerfect make creating
business documents fast and simple.
```

Margins: 1 inch
Spacing: single
Drills: 2 times

Goals:
To key 39 wam/5'/5e; to format a letter of application.

M. STARTING A LESSON

If you use the software correlated with this program, the software will direct you in completing each part of the lesson. If you are not using the software, follow the directions given with each lesson.

Each lesson heading includes instructions that tell you what software settings to use to format your document. Unless told otherwise, use 1-inch side margins and single spacing (usually the default settings). For example, the instructions in the left margin tell you to use 1-inch margins, single spacing, and to key each drill line 2 times. The goals for this lesson are to key 39 wam (words a minute) on a 5-minute timed writing with no more than 5 errors and to format a letter of application.

N. BUILDING STRAIGHT-COPY SKILL

Speed	Accuracy
aw awaken awhile	aw awaken awhile
aw awaken awhile	se severe seized
se severe seized	rd ordeal burden
se severe seized	aw awaken awhile
rd ordeal burden	se severe seized
rd ordeal burden	rd ordeal burden

Warmups. Beginning with Lesson 15, each lesson or unit starts with a 3-line warmup paragraph. All alphabet and number keys are included, as well as several common symbols. Key the Warmup twice or take three 1-minute timed writings on the paragraph.

Back-of-Book Drills. In addition to the specially constructed drills contained within the lessons, you will frequently be asked to turn to a specific drill in the back of the book for individualized practice on the passage most appropriate for your skill level. Always start at the point where you left off the previous time.

Pretest/Practice/Posttest Routines. When practicing P/P/P drills, your practice routine depends on whether you reached your accuracy goal on the Pretest. If you did, emphasize speed by keying each *individual* drill the specified number of times. If you did not reach your speed goal, emphasize accuracy by keying each *group* of lines (as though it were a paragraph) the specified number of times. These two practice routines are illustrated in the left margin.

O. MEASURING STRAIGHT-COPY SKILL

```
          20                  21
20       Ethical people sh
              24
21 they say and what they
              28
22 are in the best intere
                    32
23 should always try to a
     35               36
24 in an ethical manner.
```

All timed writings in the text are the exact length needed to reach the speed goal that is set for each lesson or unit. Thus, if you finish the timed writing, you know you have reached your speed goal.

All timed writings in the same course (that is, in the Basic, Intermediate, and Advanced courses) are of equivalent difficulty as measured by syllabic intensity (the average number of syllables per word). Thus, you can be sure that any change in your speed is due to a change in your skill rather than a change in the difficulty level of the timed writing.

If you use the software correlated with this program, your timed writings will be automatically scored for you. Your speed on a timed writing is the number of words you keyed divided by the number of minutes you keyed. Round off a fraction to the nearest whole number.

All timed writings in this book contain small numbers, called speed markers, above the copy. When you take a 5-minute timed writing, the highest number that you pass is your *wam* (words-a-minute) speed.

In addition to the timed writings in the lessons and units, the back of the book contains eight additional timed writings that may be used at any time for additional skill measurement.

P. BUILDING FORMATTING SKILL

↓ 2 inches

→4 inches Mr. Edward Whitman
Smith & Whitman Inc.
1047 Fifth Avenue
New York, NY 10028

Leave 1 space between state and ZIP Code

Marginal notes and arrows are sometimes used to remind you of margins, spacing, and so on. These aids are gradually reduced as you gain experience in formatting each kind of job.

Some jobs have special explanations which are positioned as close to the point of use as possible. Always look for and read any marginal notes before you begin to key.

Horizontal arrows (→) indicate the point at which to begin keying. For example, → 4 inches means to begin keying 4 inches from the left edge of the page (the status line should indicate Pos 4"). Down arrows (↓) indicate how far down the page a line should be keyed. For example, ↓2 inches means to begin keying 2 inches from the top edge of the page (the status line should indicate Ln 2"). Likewise, ↓4 means to press Enter 4 times before keying the next line.

Q. KEYBOARDING TECHNIQUE

Assuming the correct position at the computer enables you to key with greater speed and accuracy and less fatigue. When keying for long periods of time, rest your eyes periodically by looking away from the screen, shifting your position, or moving about.

To the extent possible, adjust your work station as follows:

Chair. Adjust the chair height so that your upper and lower legs form a 90 degree angle and your lower back is supported by the back of the chair.

Keyboard. Center your body opposite the J key, leaning forward slightly. Keep your forearms horizontal and raise your hands slightly when keying so that your wrists do not touch the keyboard or desk.

Screen. Position the monitor so that the top of the screen is just below eye level, about 18 to 26 inches away.

Text. Position your textbook (or other copy) on either side of the monitor as close to the monitor vertically and horizontally as possible to minimize head and eye movements and to avoid neck strain.

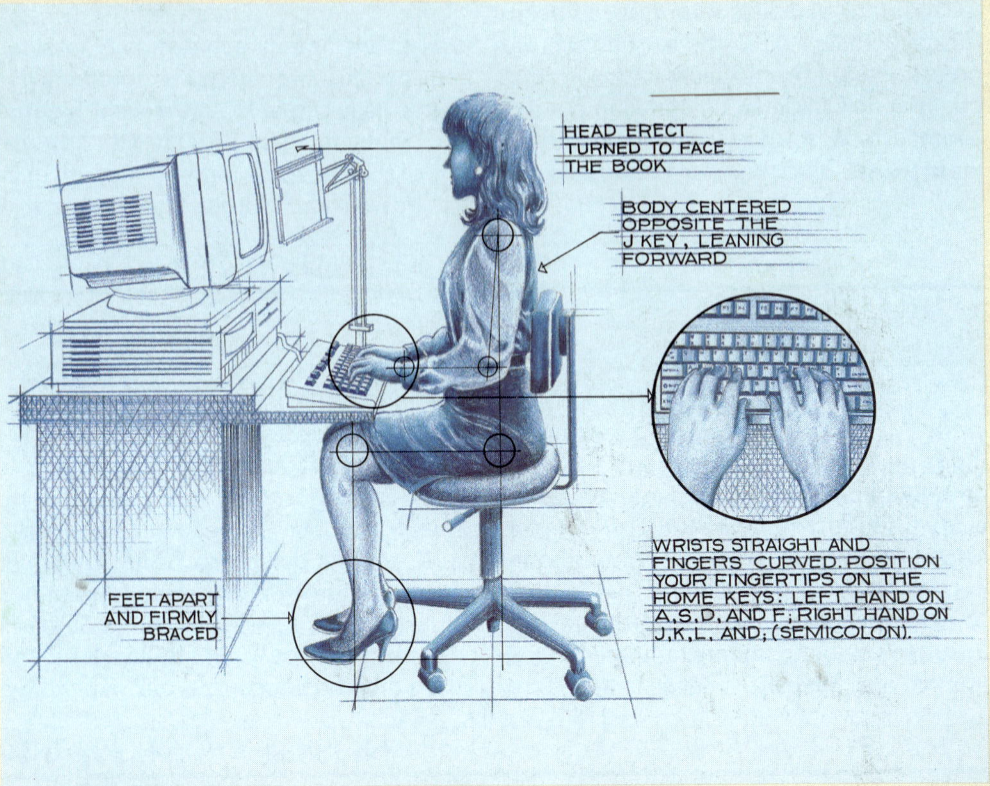

PART 1

THE ALPHABET, NUMBER, AND SYMBOL KEYS

OBJECTIVES

KEYBOARDING

To operate the letter, number, and symbol keys by touch.

To make all machine adjustments needed: set margins (if default margins are not used), tabs, and line spacing.

To key 28 words a minute on a 2-minute timed writing with no more than 5 errors.

LANGUAGE ARTS

To divide words correctly.

To proofread documents and correct errors.

To use quotation marks correctly.

WORD PROCESSING

To use the following WordPerfect commands: Line Spacing, Tab Set, Hyphenation, Underlining, Reveal Codes, and Blocking Text.

SKILLBUILDING

D. SYMBOL PRACTICE

12 Al said, "Stop it at once!" He's selling 5 @ $6.
13 Brown & Daughters held their annual Dollar Sales.
14 Julie's article* was reprinted in Newsweek today.
15 "Can't I read Catcher in the Rye?" asked Rob Lee.

E. KEYING IN ALL CAPS

Use the A finger.

To key in all-capital letters:

1. Depress the caps lock key.
2. Key the word or words.
3. Release the caps lock by pressing the caps lock key.

E. Key each sentence on a separate line.

Remember to shift for ?, !, and :.

16 Is MABEL going? Attend the MINNESOTA STATE FAIR.
17 NO SMOKING! STOP IT! Post the sign, NO HUNTING.
18 Are there EXIT and ENTRANCE signs? DO NOT ENTER.
19 An ad read: SPEND YOUR VACATION IN NORTH DAKOTA.

F. PRETEST: ALTERNATE- AND ONE-HAND WORDS

PRETEST. Take a 1-minute timed writing; compute your speed and count errors.

20 The chairman should handle their tax problem 10
21 downtown. If they are reversed, pressure tactics 20
22 might have changed the case as it was being held. 30

| 1 | 2 | 3 | 4 | 5 | 6 | 7 | 8 | 9 | 10

G. PRACTICE: ALTERNATE-HAND WORDS

PRACTICE. Speed Emphasis: If you made 2 or fewer errors on the Pretest, key each line twice.
Accuracy Emphasis: If you made 3 or more errors, key each group of lines (as though it were a paragraph) twice.

23 the with girl right blame handle antique chairman
24 for wish town their panel formal problem downtown
25 sit work make tight amend profit element neighbor
26 pan busy they flair signs thrown signals problems

H. PRACTICE: ONE-HAND WORDS

27 lip fact yolk poplin yummy affect reverse pumpkin
28 you cast kill uphill jumpy grease wagered opinion
29 tea cage lump limply hilly served bravest minimum
30 fat tree only unhook jolly garage reserve million

I. POSTTEST: ALTERNATE- AND ONE-HAND WORDS

POSTTEST. Repeat the Pretest (F) and compare performance.

J. 2-MINUTE TIMED WRITING

J. Spacing: double. Take two 2-minute timed writings. Compute your speed and count errors.

Goal: 28 wam/2'/5e

31 The purpose for all the new technology is to 10
32 make workers more productive. If this happens, a 20
33 decrease in the number of hours on the job may be 30
34 noticed. This could mean that workers would have 40
35 extra time off. This could be quite a benefit to 50
36 a large number of those workers. 56

| 1 | 2 | 3 | 4 | 5 | 6 | 7 | 8 | 9 | 10

LESSON 1 Home Keys

Margins: 1 inch • Spacing: Single • Drills: 2 times

Goals:
To control the home keys (A S D F J K L ;), the enter key, and the space bar.

A. THE HOME KEYS

The A S D F J K L ; keys are known as the home keys. Place your fingers on the home keys as follows. **Left hand:** first finger on F; second finger on D; third finger on S; fourth finger on A. **Right hand:** first finger on J; second finger on K; third finger on L; and fourth finger on ;. Keep your fingers curved.

B. THE SPACE BAR

The space bar is used to space between words and after marks of punctuation.

With fingers held motionless on the home keys, poise your right thumb about 1/4 inch above the space bar. Tap the space bar in the center, and bounce your thumb off.

Space once (*tap the space bar once*) . . . twice (*tap the space bar twice*) . . . once . . . once . . . twice . . . once . . . twice . . . once . . . twice . . . twice

NEW KEYS

C. THE ENTER KEY

Tap the enter key twice to leave a blank line between drills.

Reach to the enter key with the fourth finger of your right hand. Keep your J finger at home. Lightly tap the enter key returning the cursor to the beginning of a new line.

Practice using the enter key until you can do so with confidence and without looking at your hands.

Space once . . . twice . . . once . . . twice . . . Enter! Home! (*return fingers to home-key position*) . . . Repeat.

D. THE F AND J KEYS

Use first fingers on F and J keys. Tap the space bar with your right thumb.

```
1 fff fff jjj jjj fff jjj ff jj ff jj f j
2 fff fff jjj jjj fff jjj ff jj ff jj f j
```

G. Keep your eyes on the copy while keying.

G. SYMBOL PRACTICE

Invoice #356 to Rice & Sons required May's reply.
My total bill was $450.65, including a tax of $7.
She (May) read How to Save Money; it costs $9.50.
Luke said, "I'll buy 1 share @ $6 and 2 @ $7.55."

H. Spacing: double. Take two 2-minute timed writings. Compute your speed and count errors.

Goal: 27 wam/2′/5e

H. 2-MINUTE TIMED WRITING

If you have plans to be an expert on a job, 10
you must first have the skills; you must possess 20
good English skills as a second requirement; and 30
a third criterion is knowing how to proofread all 40
work. Start to analyze your work with care and 50
find all errors. 54

| 1 | 2 | 3 | 4 | 5 | 6 | 7 | 8 | 9 | 10

LESSON 20 Symbols

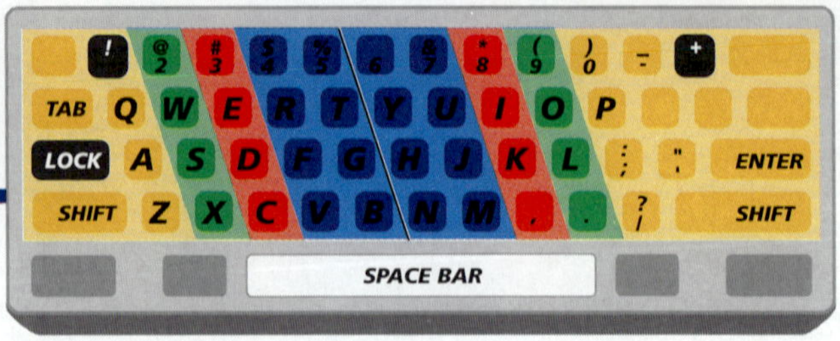

Margins: 1 inch • Tab: 0.5 inch • Spacing: Single • Drills: 2 times

Goals: To control the ! and + keys; to improve speed and accuracy; to key 28 wam/2′/5e.

A. WARMUP

Ken bought 11 prized lots @ $975. The sizes
varied but there were 3,482* (*square feet). Joe
was amazed that Ken expected to buy 12 more lots.

| 1 | 2 | 3 | 4 | 5 | 6 | 7 | 8 | 9 | 10

NEW KEYS

! 1 EXCLAMATION is the shift of 1. Use the A finger.

Space twice after an exclamation point at the end of a sentence.

+ = PLUS is the shift of EQUAL. Use the Sem finger.

Space before and after plus.

B. THE ! KEY

aqa aq1a aq!a a!!a a!!a Where! Why! How! When!
It's his! Don't do that! Stop! No! Exit Only!
He did say that! Jill can't take a vacation now!
What he said was startling! She does believe it!

C. THE + KEY

;=; ;=+; ;=+; ;++; ;++; 10 + 20 + 3 + 4 + 5 = 42.
When you add 13 + 40 + 50 + 60 + 90, you get 253.
The + sign, plus, was used in an arithmetic task.
Do you ever use the plus (+) sign in your office?

LEFT HAND			RIGHT HAND
Forefinger	F	J	Forefinger
Second Finger	D	K	Second Finger
Third Finger	S	L	Third Finger
Fourth Finger	A	;	Fourth Finger
		Space Bar	Thumb

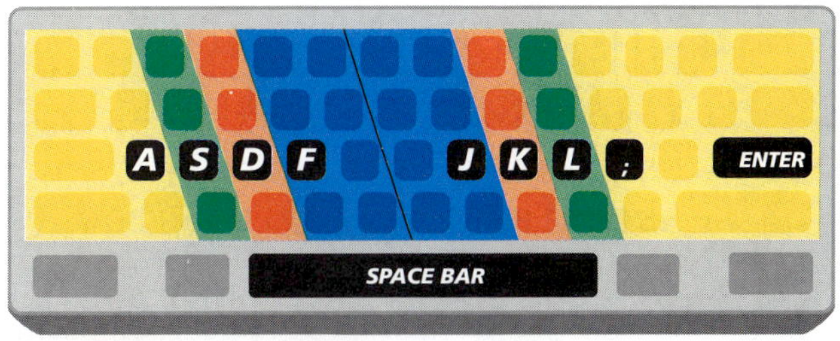

E. THE D AND K KEYS

Leave 1 blank line (strike the enter key twice) between drills.

Use second fingers on D and K. A and Sem fingers remain in home position.

```
3 ddd ddd kkk kkk ddd kkk dd kk dd kk d k
4 ddd ddd kkk kkk ddd kkk dd kk dd kk d k
```

F. THE S AND L KEYS

Use third fingers on S and L. A and Sem fingers remain on home keys.

```
5 sss sss lll lll sss lll ss ll ss ll s l
6 sss sss lll lll sss lll ss ll ss ll s l
```

G. THE A AND ; KEYS

Use fourth fingers on A and Sem. F and J fingers remain on home keys.

```
7 aaa aaa ;;; ;;; aaa ;;; aa ;; aa ;; a ;
8 aaa aaa ;;; ;;; aaa ;;; aa ;; aa ;; a ;
```

SKILLBUILDING

H. WORD BUILDING

H. Key lines 9–15 twice, leaving a blank line after each pair. Note the word patterns.

Space once after a semicolon.

```
9 aaa ddd ddd add aaa lll lll all add all
10 aaa sss kkk ask ddd aaa ddd dad ask dad
11 lll aaa ddd lad fff aaa ddd fad lad fad
12 aaa ddd ;;; ad; aaa sss ;;; ad; as; ad;
13 f fa fad fads; a as ask asks; d da dad;
14 l la las lass; f fa fal fall; s sa sad;
15 a ad add adds; l la lad lads; a ad ads;
```

I. PHRASES

I. Key lines 16–17 twice, leaving a blank line after each pair. Note the phrase patterns.

```
16 dad ask; ask a lad; dad ask a lad; as a
17 a fall; a lass; ask a lass; a lad asks;
```

J. 1-MINUTE TIMED WRITING

J. Take three 1-minute timed writings. Try to complete the line each time.

```
18 ask a sad lad; a fall fad; add a salad;
```

NEW KEYS

B. THE * KEY

ASTERISK is the shift of 8. Use the K finger.

```
4 kik ki8k k8*k k8*k k**k k**k Al's book* is great.
5 Use the * to show book/table footnote references.
6 Asterisks keyed in a row (*******) make a border.
7 Harry's* article quoted Hanson* and Pyle* in May.
```

C. THE @ KEY

AT is the shift of 2. Use the S finger.

Space before and after @.

```
8 sws sw2s s2@s s2@s s@@s s@@s Buy 15 @ $5 in June.
9 Order 12 items @ $14 and another 185 items @ $16.
10 He bought 12 units @ $14.50 and 6 units @ $12.30.
11 Buy 10 shares @ $75 and another 15 shares @ $125.
```

D. THE = KEY

EQUAL is to the right of the hyphen. Use the Sem finger.

Space before and after =.

```
12 ;=; ;=; ;==; ;==; A = 40, B = 160, C = 18, D = 1.
13 If x = 4 and y = 6 and z = 8, what is the answer?
14 He learned that A = B and was able to solve that.
15 The = sign, equal, is used by our mathematicians.
```

SKILLBUILDING

E. TECHNIQUE PRACTICE: EDITING TEXT

E. Use the WordPerfect Block command to make the necessary changes in lines 16–19.

Key lines 16–19 as shown. Then revise each line, making these changes:

1. In line 16, change *Dr.* to *Mr.* and replace *at the Holiday Hotel* with *on "Software" for me.*
2. In line 17, change *Is Tyne* to *Tyne is* and the question mark to a period.
3. In line 18, change *house* to *lot* and *March* to *October.*
4. In line 19, underline *used computer* and change *$750* to *$875.*

```
16 Dr. James Garner will speak at the Holiday Hotel.
17 Is Tyne planning an address on "Software" for me?
18 A house sold, on March 4, for less than $134,000.
19 On April 6, Jill bought a used computer for $750.
```

F. SUSTAINED PRACTICE: NUMBERS AND SYMBOLS

F. Take a 1-minute timed writing on the first paragraph to establish your base speed. Then take successive 1-minute timed writings on the other paragraphs. As soon as you equal or exceed your base speed on one paragraph, advance to the next one.

```
20      Our new store enjoyed an unexpected increase 10
21 in sales.  We were quite astonished and amazed by 20
22 the gain in numbers of customers served and kept. 30

23      We opened 18 new outlets in 14 cities, and a 10
24 catalog outlet in 29 counties.  We were then able 20
25 to serve 150,670 possible customers in 10 states. 30

26      Our gross sales were $4,560,871 (an increase 10
27 of 9%).  Knox & Sons paid $46/share and said, "It 20
28 was a great year."  These figures are confirmed.* 30
   | 1 | 2 | 3 | 4 | 5 | 6 | 7 | 8 | 9 | 10
```

LESSON 2 New Keys

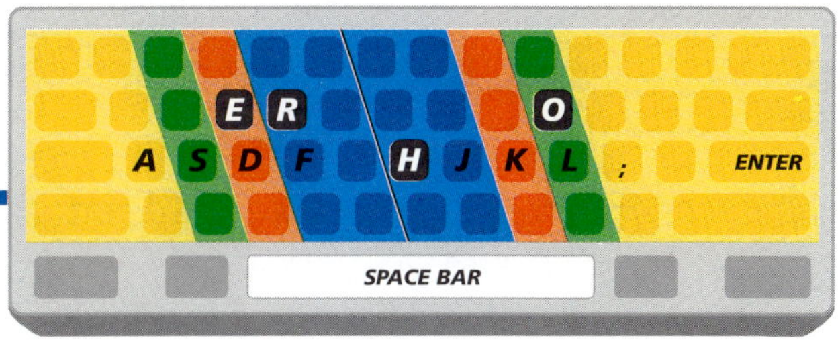

Margins: 1 inch • Spacing: Single • Drills: 2 times

Goal:
To control the H, E, O, and R keys.

Fingers are named for home keys. (Example: second finger of the left hand is the D finger.)

A. WARMUP

1 fff jjj ddd kkk sss lll aaa ;;; fff jjj
2 a salad; a lad; alas a fad; ask a lass;

NEW KEYS

B. THE H KEY

Use the J finger.

Space once after a semicolon.

3 jjj jhj jhj hjh jjj jhj jhj hjh jjj jhj
4 has has hah hah had had aha aha ash ash
5 hash half sash lash dash hall shad shah
6 as dad had; a lass has half; add a dash

C. THE E KEY

Use the D finger.

Keep your eyes on the copy as you key.

7 ddd ded ded ede ddd ded ded ede ddd ded
8 lea led see he; she eke fed sea lee fee
9 keel fake head feed seal ease lead held
10 she held a lease; he fed a seal; a keel

D. THE O KEY

Use the L finger.

Keep fingers curved.

11 lll lol lol olo lll lol lol olo lll lol
12 doe off foe hod oh; oak odd ode old sod
13 shoe look kook joke odes does solo oleo
14 he held a hook; a lass solos; old foes;

E. THE R KEY

Use the F finger.

Keep A finger at home.

15 fff frf frf rfr fff frf frf rfr fff frf
16 red ark ore err rah era rod oar her are
17 oars soar dear fare read role rare door
18 he read a rare reader; a dark red door;

SKILLBUILDING

G. Underline individual words separately; for a book title, underline the entire title, including the spaces.

G. TECHNIQUE PRACTICE: UNDERLINING

The Sindbad Voyage is an excellent story for all.
Are the words for, fore, and four used correctly?
We had an ad in The Wall Street Journal in March.
Max will not or should not attend the conference.

H. Keep your eyes on the copy so that you do not lose your place as you key these longer words.

H. CONCENTRATION PRACTICE

The provocative statement caused an insurrection.
A congregation in Connecticut intervened quickly.
A lackadaisical traveler crisscrossed continents.
All resignations were interpreted as irrevocable.

I. Spacing: double. Take two 1-minute timed writings. Compute your speed and count errors.

I. HANDWRITTEN PARAGRAPH

You will discover when you begin working in 10
industry that there are other skills you need to 20
possess beyond the basic business skills. Skills 30
in human relations are desirable for every worker. 40

J. Spacing: double. Take two 2-minute timed writings. Compute your speed and count errors.

Goal: 26 wam/2′/5e

J. 2-MINUTE TIMED WRITING

Van Clark was amazed at how quickly he could 10
key on a new computer. It took him just a little 20
time to learn the functions it can perform. He 30
expected he would surely forget how to use it his 40
first time alone, but he did not. He had learned 50
the skill. 52

| 1 | 2 | 3 | 4 | 5 | 6 | 7 | 8 | 9 | 10

LESSON 19

Symbols and Editing Text

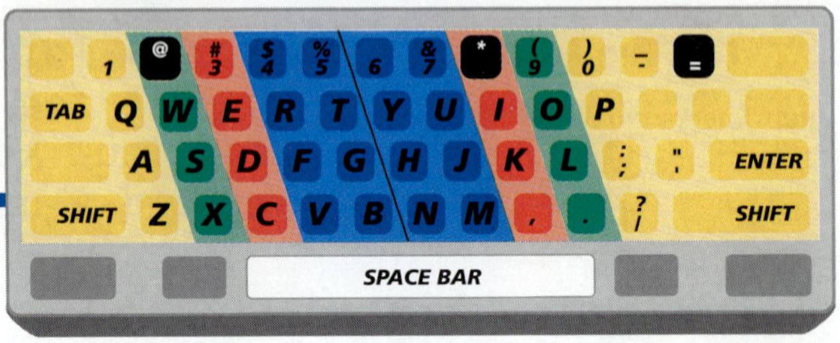

Margins: 1 inch • Tab: 0.5 inch • Spacing: Single • Drills: 2 times

Goals:
To control the *, @, and = keys; to edit text; to key 27 wam/2′/5e.

A. WARMUP

The owner (Mr. Judd) quoted a sales price of 10
$3.86 for the items. He expects Grove & Baker to 20
buy nearly 129,457 units of these sizzling items. 30

| 1 | 2 | 3 | 4 | 5 | 6 | 7 | 8 | 9 | 10

SKILLBUILDING

F. WORD FAMILIES

Do not pause at the vertical lines that mark off the word families.

19 hale sale kale dale | sold fold hold old;
20 seed heed deed feed | sash dash lash ash;
21 rake sake fake lake | rear sear dear ear;

G. 1-MINUTE TIMED WRITING

G. Take three 1-minute timed writings. Try to complete both lines each time. Use word wrap.

22 he asked for a rare old deed; she had a
23 door ajar;

LESSON 3 New Keys

Margins: 1 inch • Spacing: Single • Drills: 2 times

Goal: To control the M, T, I, and C keys.

A. WARMUP

1 aa ;; ss ll dd kk ff jj hh ee oo rr aa;
2 he held a sale for her as she had asked

NEW KEYS

B. THE M KEY

Use the J finger.

3 jjj jmj jmj mjm jjj jmj jmj mjm jjj jmj
4 mad mom me; am jam; ram dam ham ma; mar
5 same lame room fame make roam loam arms
6 she made more room for some of her ham;

C. THE T KEY

Use the F finger.

7 fff ftf ftf tft fff ftf ftf tft fff ftf
8 hot jot rat eat tam mat lot sat art tar
9 mate tool fate mart date late told take
10 he told her to set a later date to eat;

LESSON 18 Symbols

Margins: 1 inch • Tab: 0.5 inch • Spacing: Single • Drills: 2 times

Goals:
To control the &, $, and _ keys; to underline; to key 26 wam/2′/5e.

A. WARMUP

1 Of the 345 votes cast, 279 were for Jo. She 10
2 won by 81%. Jo's quick win amazed 60 of her pals 20
3 from home. The "Times" exalted the huge victory. 30

| 1 | 2 | 3 | 4 | 5 | 6 | 7 | 8 | 9 | 10

NEW KEYS

B. THE & KEY

AMPERSAND (sign for *and*) is the shift of 7. Use the J finger.

Space before and after the ampersand.

4 juj ju7j j7j j7&j j&&j j&&j Max & Dee & Sue & Ken
5 Brown & Sons shipped goods to Crum & Lee Company.
6 Johnson & Loo brought a case against May & Green.
7 Ball & Trump vs. Vens & See is being decided now.

C. THE $ KEY

DOLLAR is the shift of 4. Use the F finger.

Do not space between the dollar sign and the number.

8 frf fr4f f4f f4$f f$$f f$$f $44 $444 $4,444 $4.44
9 I quoted $48, $64, and $94 for the set of chairs.
10 His insurance paid $150; our insurance paid $175.
11 First-floor seats were $25, $30, and $55 in June.

D. THE _ KEY

UNDERLINE is the shift of the hyphen. Use the Sem finger.

Blank lines within sentences are 5 characters long.

12 ;p; ;p-; ;p-; ;p_; ;_; ;_; Use a date of _____.
13 My new hours are from _____ a.m. until _____ p.m.
14 My sales goal of $_____ is an increase of _____%.
15 There are _____ graduating; only _____ will stay.

FORMATTING

E. WORDPERFECT: BLOCK TEXT

WP

BLOCK
Alt-F4 or F12, *highlight text*

Block is used to highlight a section of text, such as a word, phrase, sentence, or paragraph. You can then perform other commands, such as underlining or deleting the block of text.

To define a block, position the cursor under the first character you wish to block and press Alt-F4 or F12. WordPerfect will display "Block On" at the bottom of your screen. Next, move the cursor to the right of the last character you wish to block. The block of text is now highlighted, and you can issue another command, such as pressing F8 to underline.

F. WORDPERFECT: UNDERLINING

WP

UNDERLINING
F8

To underline text as you key it, turn on underlining by pressing F8. Then key the text and press F8 again (or the right arrow key) to turn off underlining. To underline existing text, block the text to be underlined, then press F8.

NOTE: Do not be concerned if you make errors in these early lessons. Making errors is expected at this stage of your learning.

If you forget where a key is located, look at the keyboard chart, not at your fingers.

D. THE I KEY

Use the K finger.

11 kkk kik kik iki kkk kik kik iki kkk kik
12 air fir dim sir him rim kit sit did lid
13 iris tide site item fire idea tile tire
14 this time he left his tie at the store;

E. THE C KEY

Use the D finger.

15 ddd dcd dcd cdc ddd dcd dcd cdc ddd dcd
16 cot sac cod act car coo cat arc ice ace
17 rich tack chat face aces itch coat deck
18 he liked to race cars at the old track;

SKILLBUILDING

F. WORD FAMILIES

Sit in the correct position as you key these drills. Refer to the illustration on page OL-6.

19 sail tail rail fail | mace face lace ace;
20 dots tots jots lots | mire tire fire ire;
21 jade fade made ade; | seed deed feed heed
22 hale tale sale dale | cads lads fads ads;

G. SHORT PHRASES

23 as so | do as | if it | she is | he did | she had
24 so as | as if | it is | did it | it had | has met
25 to it | do it | if he | for it | as she | let her
26 he is | as do | of it | far as | of her | had his

H. 1-MINUTE TIMED WRITING

H. Take three 1-minute timed writings. Try to complete both lines each time. Use word wrap. Press Enter only at the end of line 28.

27 their old store had lots of deck chairs
28 for his leased home;

LANGUAGE ARTS

E. PLACEMENT OF QUOTATION MARKS

Read these rules about the placement of quotation marks. Then key lines 16–19 twice.

1. The closing quotation mark is always keyed *after* a period or comma but *before* a colon or semicolon.
2. The closing quotation mark is keyed *after* a question mark or exclamation point if the quoted material is a question or an exclamation; otherwise, the quotation mark is keyed *before* the question mark or exclamation point.

16 "Hello," I said. "My name is Al; I am new here."

17 Zack read the article "Can She Succeed Tomorrow?"

18 John said, "I'll mail the check"; but, he didn't.

19 Did he say, "We lost"? She said, "I don't know."

SKILLBUILDING

F. ALPHABET AND SYMBOL PRACTICE

20 Gaze at views of my jonquil or red phlox in back.

21 Jan quickly moved the six dozen big pink flowers.

22 Joe quietly picked six razors from the woven bag.

23 Packing jam for the dozen boxes was quite lively.

24 Mail these "Rush": #38, #89, and #99 (software).

25 Joe's note carried a rate of 6%; Ann's only 5.5%.

26 Lee read "The Computer Today." It's here Monday.

27 Ask (1) Tom, (2) Dick, and (3) Harry (Feigleson).

G. Spacing: double. Set tabs every 1.2 inches. Press tab to begin the first column.

G. TECHNIQUE PRACTICE: TAB KEY

28	perfect	agency	office	disc
29	security	company	employer	firm
30	Monday	workers	vacation	employee
31	also	wouldn't	it's	computer

H. Spacing: double. Take two 1-minute timed writings. Compute your speed and count errors.

H. HANDWRITTEN PARAGRAPHS

32 You have now completed the first sequence of 10

33 your class and have learned how to make the right 20

34 reaches to those alpha, numeric, and symbol keys. 30

35 In the next sequence, you will be taught how 40

36 to center and to develop your keyboarding skills. 50

I. Spacing: double. Take two 2-minute timed writings. Compute your speed and count errors.

Goal: 25 wam/2′/5e

I. 2-MINUTE TIMED WRITING

37 We can expect quite a few changes in our job 10

38 market in the next few decades. People will have 20

39 jobs that will require new tasks due to the many 30

40 uses of the computer. We will have a gain in the 40

41 size of the labor force which processes our data. 50

| 1 | 2 | 3 | 4 | 5 | 6 | 7 | 8 | 9 | 10

LESSON 4 New Keys

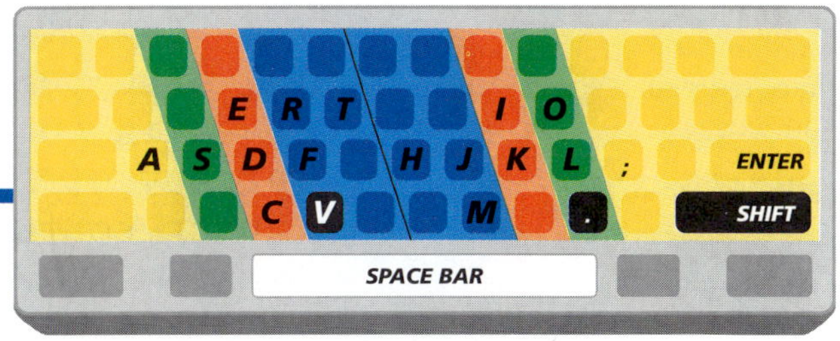

Margins: 1 inch • Spacing: Single • Drills: 2 times

Goals:
To control the right shift, V, and period keys; to count errors.

A. WARMUP

1 the farmer hired her to feed the mares;
2 the first callers came to see the iris;

NEW KEYS

B. THE RIGHT SHIFT KEY

To capitalize letters on the left half of the keyboard:
1. With the J finger at home, press and hold down the right shift key with the Sem finger.
2. Strike the letter key.
3. Release the shift key and return fingers to home position.

3 ;;; ;A; ;A; ;;; ;S; ;S; ;;; ;D; ;D; ;;;
4 Art Alf Sal Tom Sam Dee Ted Rae Sam Ada
5 Chet Edie Elsa Carl Amos Todd Sara Dick
6 Sara Edie Carter married Carl Sam Amos;

C. THE V KEY

Use the F finger.

7 fff fvf fvf vfv fff fvf fvf vfv fff fvf
8 Val eve Eva via vim vis Viv vet Ava vie
9 live have Vida ever vast Vera move vote
10 Victor Vida moved to Vassar to see Val;

D. . KEY

Use the L finger.

Space once after a period following an abbreviation; none after a period within an abbreviation; twice after a period ending a sentence.

11 lll l.l l.l .l. lll l.l l.l .l. lll l.l
12 sr. sr. dr. dr. ea. ea. Dr. Dr. Sr. Sr.
13 misc. D.C. jr. A.D. loc. cit. i.e. a.m.
14 Eva left. David came. Elsa came home.

SKILLBUILDING

E. PHRASES

15 as some | let him | are so | has had | ask them
16 to move | see her | for it | had the | did some
17 do have | her old | did he | jot the | had this
18 so ever | let her | she is | see him | for them

J. Spacing: double. Take two 2-minute timed writings. Compute your speed and count errors.

Goal: 24 wam/2′/5e

J. 2-MINUTE TIMED WRITING

```
     The personal computer has changed all of our  10
lives in just a few years.  Since we have quite a  20
variety of software programs for our use, we can   30
expect to find that a computer will let us do an   40
amazing amount of work in less time than before.   48
| 1 | 2 | 3 | 4 | 5 | 6 | 7 | 8 | 9 | 10
```

LESSON 17 Symbols

Margins: 1 inch • Tab: 0.5 inch • Spacing: Single • Drills: 2 times

Goals:
To control the %, ′, and ″ keys; to key 25 wam/2′/5e.

A. WARMUP

```
     Jack Xua quizzed the men about 345# of grain  10
(wheat) found by 26 boys on Lot #98.  Two men had  20
paid 17 students to place the wheat in 20# units.  30
| 1 | 2 | 3 | 4 | 5 | 6 | 7 | 8 | 9 | 10
```

NEW KEYS

B. THE % KEY

PERCENT is the shift of 5. Use the F finger.

Do not space between the number and the percent sign.

```
ft5f ft5%f f5%f f5%f f%%f f%%f 5% 55% 555% 5,555%
Robert quoted rates of 8%, 9%, 10%, 11%, and 12%.
Pat scored 82%, Jan 89%, and Ken 90% on the test.
Only 55% of the students passed 75% of the exams.
```

C. THE ' KEY

APOSTROPHE is to the right of the semicolon. Use the Sem finger.

```
;'; ''' ;'; '''  Can't we go in Sue's or Al's car?
It's Bob's job to cover Ted's work when he's out.
What's in Mike's lunch box for Stanley's dessert?
He's left for Ty's banquet which is held at Al's.
```

D. THE " KEY

QUOTATION is the shift of the apostrophe. Use the Sem finger.

Do not space between the quotation marks and the text they enclose.

```
;'; """" ;"; """" "That's a super job," said Mabel.
The theme of the meeting is "Improving Your Job."
Jill liked "Grand Hotel"; Sharon liked "Fiddler."
Allison said, "I'll take Janice and Jo to Flint."
```

F. COUNTING ERRORS

Count an error when:

1. Any stroke is incorrect.
2. Any punctuation after a word is incorrect or omitted. Count the word before the punctuation.
3. The spacing after a word or after its punctuation is incorrect. Count the word as incorrect.
4. A letter or word is omitted.
5. A letter or word is repeated.
6. A direction about spacing, indenting, and so on, is violated.
7. Words are transposed.

Note: Only one error is counted for each word, no matter how many errors it may contain.

Compare the copy with lines 19–21 below.

```
Ada mailwd a letter; Dee mailed a card.                 [1]
Ada mailed a letter. Dee mailed a card.                 [2]
Dell soldsome  of the food to a market.                 [3]
Dell sold som the food to to a market.                  [4] [5]
 Alma asked for Dick three more tickets.                [6] [7]
Alma asked Dick for three more tockits.
```

G. SENTENCES

G. After keying each line 2 times, count your errors.

19 Ada mailed a letter; Dee mailed a card.
20 Dell sold some of the food to a market.
21 Alma asked Dick for three more tickets.

H. 1-MINUTE TIMED WRITING

H. Take three 1-minute timed writings. Try to complete both lines each time.

22 Vic asked them to tell the major to see
23 Carla at the local firm.

LESSON 5 Review

Margins: 1 inch • Spacing: Single • Drills: 2 times

Goals: To reinforce new-key reaches; to compute speed.

A. WARMUP

1 Val called Dale to ask for a ride home.
2 Edie took three old jars to her mother.

E. Select the words in each line that can be divided, and key them with a hyphen to show where the division should be (Example: *con-sult*).

E. WORD DIVISION PRACTICE

dragged	weren't	today
safety	moment	USMC
grandmother	teenagers	trailing
expect	reproach	couldn't

WP

HYPHENATION—AUTOMATIC
Sh-F8, 1, 1, Y, F7

HYPHENATION PROMPT

Position the cursor at division point, Ctrl-Hyphen

F. WORDPERFECT: HYPHENATION

Use Hyphenation to maintain a more even right margin. WordPerfect will automatically divide most words correctly. If it needs help, a screen prompt will ask you to position the hyphen (use the arrow keys) at a correct division point; then press Esc. If the word should not be hyphenated, press F1.

To manually divide a word not in WordPerfect's dictionary, position the cursor at the division point and press Ctrl-Hyphen.

G. Key the paragraph with Hyphenation on.

G. HYPHENATION PRACTICE

In order for you to become a part of the
emerging telecommunications field, your course of
study must consist of a preponderance of courses
in that field. Not keeping up with technological
advances could hurt your career.

SKILLBUILDING

H. Take a 1-minute timed writing on the first paragraph to establish your base speed. Then take successive 1-minute timed writings on the other paragraphs. As soon as you equal or exceed your base speed on one paragraph, advance to the next one.

H. SUSTAINED PRACTICE: SYLLABIC INTENSITY

One should always try to keep in good shape. 10
As the first step in keeping in good shape, avoid 20
starting or being tempted with the smoking habit. 30

A second step that helps in maintaining good 10
health for years is drinking the proper amount of 20
water. Most doctors suggest eight glasses a day. 30

Making exercise a step is another method for 10
staying in good health. Many experts suggest one 20
spend a few minutes each day in regular exercise. 30

A final step of importance is maintaining an 10
appropriate body weight. The clue to maintaining 20
weight is developing the positive eating pattern. 30

| 1 | 2 | 3 | 4 | 5 | 6 | 7 | 8 | 9 | 10

I. Spacing: double. Take two 1-minute timed writings. Compute your speed and count errors.

I. HANDWRITTEN PARAGRAPHS WITH NUMBERS

The membership in our credit union is 1,850. 10
We need 200 new members if we are to reach 2,050. 20
There were 46 new members in May, 33 in June, and 30
24 in July for a total of 103. If we are to have 40
93 new members, it means we must get started now. 50

SKILLBUILDING

B. WORD FAMILIES

```
3 lace face mace race | fame tame lame same
4 mail tail sail rail | fold cold mold told
5 mate late date fate | feed seed deed heed
```

C. PHRASES

```
6 or there | did he | for the | some mail | is he
7 is after | has it | ask the | come home | if it
8 he liked | she is | did she | late date | he is
9 it faces | had he | her hat | same mail | as if
```

D. If you are using the software that comes with this course, your speed will be computed automatically.

D. COMPUTING SPEED

Compare with line 12.

```
Carl asked him to deed the farm to Ted.
Carl asked him to deed the farm to Ted.
Carl asked
| 1 | 2 | 3 | 4 | 5 | 6 | 7 | 8
```

Compare with lines 13–15.

```
Della asked David to take her to school
for a short time.  She had to meet Fred
or Sarah at the school office at three.
Della asked David to
| 1 | 2 | 3 | 4 | 5 | 6 | 7 | 8
```

Keyboarding speed is measured in words a minute (wam). To compute wam, count every 5 strokes, including spaces, as 1 "word." Horizontal word scales (see E) divide lines into 5-stroke words. In paragraph copy, words are cumulatively totaled at the end of each line (see F).

In Example 1, speed is 18 wam (8 + 8 + 2). In Example 2, speed is 28 wam (24 + 4). For timed writings other than a minute, divide the number of words keyed by the number of minutes in the timed writing. For example, if you key 28 words in 2 minutes, your speed is 14 wam (28 ÷ 2); in 1 minute, 28 wam (28 ÷ 1); or in 1/2 minute, 56 wam (28 ÷ 1/2).

E. Take a 1-minute timed writing on each line. Compute your speed and count errors.

E. SENTENCES

```
10 Vickie loved the fame she had achieved.
11 Art dashed to take the jet to his home.
12 Carl asked him to deed the farm to Ted.
   | 1 | 2 | 3 | 4 | 5 | 6 | 7 | 8        = 5-stroke words
```

F. Take two 1-minute timed writings on the paragraph. Press Enter only at the end of the paragraph. Compute your speed and count errors.

F. PARAGRAPH

```
                                              CUMULATIVE WORDS
13 Della asked David to take her to school     8
14 for a short time.  She had to meet Fred    16
15 or Sarah at the school office at three.    24
   | 1 | 2 | 3 | 4 | 5 | 6 | 7 | 8
```

G. Take three 1-minute timed writings. Compute your speed and count errors.

G. 1-MINUTE TIMED WRITING

```
16 Cass said she asked Al Rice to meet her     8
17 at five to look for a jacket.              14
   | 1 | 2 | 3 | 4 | 5 | 6 | 7 | 8
```

LESSON 16 Symbols and Word Division

Margins: 1 inch • Tab: 0.5 inch • Spacing: Single • Drills: 2 times

Goals:
To control the #, (, and) keys; to make correct word-division decisions; to key 24 wam/2'/5e.

A. WARMUP

1   Fay Jacobs drove 1,568 miles last week. She 10
2 met 39 aides in Arizona and Oregon. She expected 20
3 and required a 4:20 meeting with 17 new managers. 30

| 1 | 2 | 3 | 4 | 5 | 6 | 7 | 8 | 9 | 10

NEW KEYS

B. THE # KEY

NUMBER (if before a figure) or POUNDS (if after a figure) is the shift of 3. Use the D finger.

Do not space between the figure and symbol.

4 de3d de3#d d3#d d3#d d##d d##d #3 #33 #333 #3,333
5 Al wants 33# of #200 and 38# of #400 by Saturday.
6 My favorite seats are #2, #34, #56, #65, and #66.
7 Please order 45# of #245 and 13# of #24 tomorrow.

C. THE (AND) KEYS

PARENTHESES are the shifts of 9 and 0. Use the L finger on (and the Sem finger on).

Do not space between the parentheses and the text within them.

8 lo91 lo91 lo(1 lo(1 l((l ;p0; ;p0; ;p); ;p); ;));
9 Please ask (1) Al, (2) Pat, (3) Ted, and (4) Dee.
10 Sue has some (1) skis, (2) sleds, and (3) skates.
11 Mary is (1) prompt, (2) speedy, and (3) accurate.

12 Our workers (Lewis, Jerry, and Ty) were rewarded.
13 The owner (Ms. Parks) went on Friday (August 18).
14 The Roxie (a cafe) had fish (salmon) on the menu.
15 The clerk (Ms. Fay Green) will vote yes (not no).

LANGUAGE ARTS

D. WORD DIVISION

Whenever you key material with word wrap off, you must decide where each line should end.

If it is necessary to divide a word, follow the rules given here.

1. Do not divide (*a*) words pronounced as one syllable (*thought, planned*), (*b*) contractions (*isn't, shouldn't*), or (*c*) abbreviations (*ILGWU, Inc.*).
2. Divide words only between syllables. Whenever you are unsure of where a syllable ends, consult a dictionary.
3. Leave at least three characters (the last will be a hyphen) on the upper line, and carry at least three characters (the last may be a punctuation mark) to the next line. Thus, *al-ways* and *mat-ter,* but not *a-round* or *trick-y.*
4. Divide compound words either at the hyphen (*self-control*) or where the two words join to make a solid compound. Thus *master-mind,* not *mas-termind.*

LESSON 6 New Keys

Margins: 1 inch • Spacing: Single • Drills: 2 times

Goals:
To control the N, W, comma, and G keys; to key 15 wam/1′/3e.

"15 wam/1′/3e" means to key at the rate of 15 words a minute for 1 minute with no more than 3 errors.

A. WARMUP

1 A major firm sold office items at cost.
2 Viola had her office clerks assist her.

NEW KEYS

B. THE N KEY

Use the J finger.

Keep other fingers at home as you reach to N.

3 jjj jnj jnj njn jjj jnj jnj njn jjj jnj
4 man fan ran sin den kin tin tan and not
5 sane rain even cent find seen then none
6 Dan and Al can enter the main entrance.

C. THE W KEY

Use the S finger.

7 sss sws sws wsw sss sws sws wsw sss sws
8 now two tow how wow row who law few saw
9 want will when wine warm wait saws wave
10 Walt Shaw will want to walk with Wanda.

D. THE , KEY

Use the K finger.

Space once after a comma.

11 kkk k,k k,k ,k, kkk k,k k,k ,k, kkk k,k
12 or, of, to, oh, it, no, if, is, so, do,
13 too, if it is, as soon as, if so, what,
14 Dale, Annie, Sadie, and Edith left too.

E. THE G KEY

Use the F finger.

Keep wrists low, but not resting on keyboard.

15 fff fgf fgf gfg fff fgf fgf gfg fff fgf
16 log rag egg age nag tag sag get leg got
17 sage grow rage wing grew gown wage gain
18 Gail greeted the Garden Town Gardeners.

C. Spacing: double. Set multiple left tabs every 1.2 inches. Press tab to begin the first column.

C. TECHNIQUE PRACTICE: ALIGN WORDS LEFT

dear	business	loan	office
computer	disk	yours	sincerely
keying	budget	our	employees

D. Spacing: double. Set multiple right tabs every 1.5 inches. Clear existing tabs before setting new tabs. Change the Ls to Rs for right tabs.

D. TECHNIQUE PRACTICE: ALIGN NUMBERS RIGHT

109	780,331	10,456	1
9,456	67	273	8,780
33	1,489	410,345	105

E. Spacing: double. Decimal tabs every 1.5 inches. Clear existing tabs before setting new tabs. Change the Ls to Ds for dec tabs.

E. TECHNIQUE PRACTICE: ALIGN DECIMALS

.05	10.33	100.25	1.6
9.25	133.66	1,345.66	100.67
106.09	1.333	.025	56.89

SKILLBUILDING

PRETEST.
Take a 1-minute timed writing; compute your speed and count errors.

F. PRETEST: VERTICAL REACHES

A few of our business managers attribute the 10
success of the bank to a judicious and scientific 20
reserve program. The bank cannot drop its guard. 30

| 1 | 2 | 3 | 4 | 5 | 6 | 7 | 8 | 9 | 10

PRACTICE.
Speed Emphasis: If you made 2 or fewer errors on the Pretest, key each line twice.
Accuracy Emphasis: If you made 3 or more errors, key each group of lines (as though it were a paragraph) twice.

G. PRACTICE: UP REACHES

at atlas plate water later batch fatal match late
dr draft drift drums drawn drain drama dress drab
ju jumpy juror junky jumbo julep judge juice just
es essay press bless crest quest fresh rises less

H. PRACTICE: DOWN REACHES

ca cable cabin cadet camel cameo candy carve cash
nk trunk drink prank rinks brink drank crank sink
ba batch badge bagel baked banjo barge basis bank
sc scale scald scrub scalp scare scout scarf scan

POSTTEST.
Repeat the Pretest (F) and compare performance.

I. POSTTEST: VERTICAL REACHES

J. Spacing: double. Take two 2-minute timed writings. Compute your speed and count errors.

Goal: 23 wam/2'/5e

J. 2-MINUTE TIMED WRITING

One of the reasons for all the technology is 10
to help us become more productive. If this does 20
happen, we would have an amazing amount of extra 30
time off. Quite a few of our job skills would be 40
changed to meet new standards. 46

| 1 | 2 | 3 | 4 | 5 | 6 | 7 | 8 | 9 | 10

SKILLBUILDING

F. TECHNIQUE PRACTICE: SPACE BAR

19 Al is here. Ed is fine. Cal can meet.
20 Do it. See them. Rae did. Del is it.
21 Dora is home. Fred went. Cal is here.
22 Take the tram. Ed is in. Art is home.
23 Walt is there. Edith lost it. She is.

G. Take two 1-minute timed writings. Compute your speed and count errors.

G. 1-MINUTE TIMED WRITING

	WORDS
24 Ted joined the firm one month ago. Ted	8
25 will see Valerie for a review too.	15
| 1 | 2 | 3 | 4 | 5 | 6 | 7 | 8	

7 LESSON New Keys

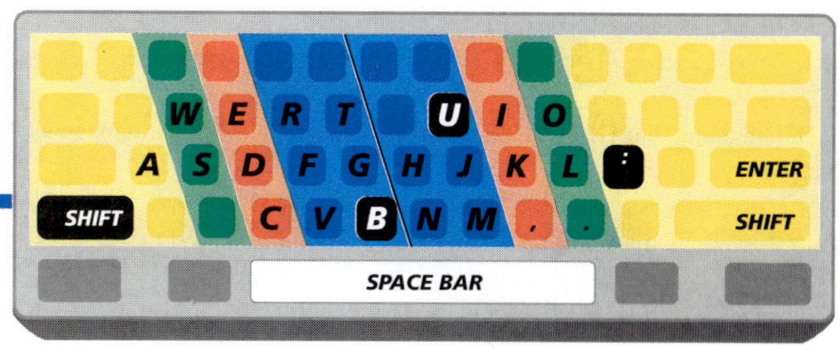

Margins: 1 inch • Spacing: Single • Drills: 2 times

Goals:
To control the left shift, U, B, and colon keys; to key 16 wam/1′/3e.

A. WARMUP

1 Evie jogged more than a mile with Walt.
2 Will Shea joined the Georgia Five team.

NEW KEYS

To capitalize letters on the right half of the keyboard:
1. With the F finger at home, press and hold down the left shift key with the A finger.
2. Strike the letter key.
3. Release the shift key and return fingers to home position.

B. THE LEFT SHIFT KEY

3 aaa Jaa Jaa aaa Kaa Kaa aaa Laa Laa aaa
4 Lee Joe Kim Ira Hal Ned Kit Mel Ken Jed
5 John Hans Mark Nita Iris Kate Hank Lian
6 Kate Mace went with Ned Hall to Kenton.

Use the J finger.

Keep other fingers at home as you reach to U.

C. THE U KEY

7 jjj juj juj uju jjj juj juj uju jjj juj
8 dug cue rut run due jug sue lug sun urn
9 just hulk nuns dunk sulk hums must junk
10 Hugh Unger urged that Hugo must unload.

G. Spacing: double. Take two 1-minute timed writings. Compute your speed and count errors.

G. HANDWRITTEN PARAGRAPH

Jobs in business require good skills in oral 10
and written communications. Confirmation of this 20
fact can be found in various magazines and books. 30

H. Spacing: double. Take two 2-minute timed writings. Compute your speed and count errors.

Goal: 22 wam/2′/5e

H. 2-MINUTE TIMED WRITING

New equipment is letting us share more and 10
more data in less time than ever. Experts tell 20
us if we link phones and computers, we could have 30
data that will quickly zoom from site to site to 40
help all jobholders. 44

| 1 | 2 | 3 | 4 | 5 | 6 | 7 | 8 | 9 | 10

LESSON 15 Review

Margins: 1 inch • Tab: 0.5 inch • Spacing: Single • Drills: 2 times

Goals:
To key 23 wam/2′/5e; to set tabs; to align text right and left; to align decimals.

A. WARMUP

Hazel Jacobson asked the attendant what time 10
Flight 948 was expected to arrive in Quincy. She 20
said probably at 2:30 or 2:35 at Gate 16A or 17B. 30

| 1 | 2 | 3 | 4 | 5 | 6 | 7 | 8 | 9 | 10

FORMATTING

WP

TAB SET
Sh-F8, 1, 8, *tab position,* Enter F7, F7

Clear all tabs: Ctrl-End

Set tabs in spaces rather than inches: *tab position,* U

Set multiple tabs: *tab position for first tab, comma, amount of space between tabs*

B. WORDPERFECT: TAB SET

WordPerfect has default tabs set every 0.5 inch (5 spaces). Pressing the tab key moves the cursor 0.5 inch to the right.

Enter the appropriate commands to access the tab ruler (Sh-F8, 1, 8). To clear the default tabs, position the cursor at the beginning of the line and press Ctrl-End; to clear an individual tab, position the cursor under the tab and press Delete.

To set a left tab (indicated by the letter "L"), enter the position number (e.g., "0.5") and press Enter. You must enter 0 (zero) and a decimal point before any number less than 1. To set a tab in terms of spaces rather than inches, enter "U" (for units) after the number (e.g., "3u" for a tab 3 spaces from the left margin).

To set tabs at regular intervals, enter the position number for the first tab, a comma, and the amount of space between tabs (e.g., "0,1.5" for tabs 1.5 inches apart beginning at the left margin).

To set a right tab (for aligning at the right), enter the position number, press Enter, then change L to R. To set a decimal or dec tab (for aligning at the decimal point), enter the position number, press Enter, then change L to D.

D. THE B KEY

Use the F finger.

11 fff fbf fbf bfb fff fbf fbf bfb fff fbf
12 big orb cab bun bow bid bit bin bag job
13 bush back bask bulb bent bunt blew bend
14 Bob backed Bill in a bid for a big job.

E. THE : KEY

The colon is the shift of the semicolon key.

Use the Sem finger.

Space once after a period following an abbreviation; twice after a colon.

15 ;;; ;:; ;:; :;: ;;; ;:; ;:; :;: ;;; ;:;
16 Mr. Uhl: Mrs. Low: Dr. Roe: Ms. See:
17 Dear Mrs. Mills: Dear John: Dear Lee:
18 Date: To: From: Subject: as listed:

SKILLBUILDING

F. KEYBOARD PRACTICE

Top row

19 We were told to take our truck to Hugo.
20 There were two tired men waiting there.
21 Write to their hometown to inform them.

Home row

22 Jake asked his dad for small red flags.
23 Sara added a dash of salt to the salad.
24 Dale said she had a fall sale in Elson.

Bottom row

25 He can come at five for nine old canes.
26 Burton came to vote with vim and vigor.
27 Bob had nerve to come via a Boston bus.

G. 1-MINUTE TIMED WRITING

G. Take two 1-minute timed writings. Compute your speed and count errors.

Goal: 16 wam/1′/3e

	WORDS
28 Dear Jack: Fred would like to take Ben	8
29 and us to a home game at five tomorrow.	16
| 1 | 2 | 3 | 4 | 5 | 6 | 7 | 8	

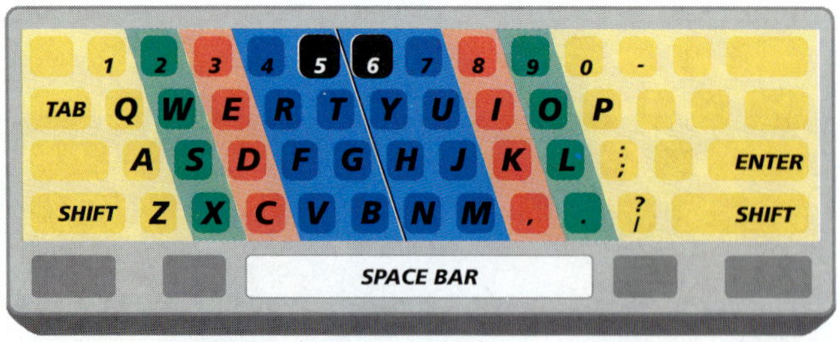

NEW KEYS

B. THE 5 KEY

Use the F finger.

4 fr5f fr5f f55f f55f f5f5 f5f5 5 55 555 5,555 5:55
5 55 fury 55 foes 55 fibs 55 fads 55 furs 55 favors
6 The 55 students read the 555 pages in 55 minutes.
7 She found Items 5, 10, and 29; I found 47 and 38.

C. THE 6 KEY

Use the J finger.

8 jy6j jy6j j66j j66j j6j6 j6j6 6 66 666 6,666 6:66
9 66 jots 66 jams 66 jump 66 jabs 66 join 66 jewels
10 Tom Lux left at 6:16 on Train 66 to go 600 miles.
11 There were 53,640 people in Bath; 28,179 in Hale.

SKILLBUILDING

D. NUMBER PRACTICE: 5 AND 6

12 The 65 adults went to 5566 Wooster Avenue on 6/5.
13 On 5/6 at the age of 6, Andrew weighed 55 pounds.
14 If Gail takes 10 percent of 650, she will get 65.
15 Call Jeffrey at 555-8407 or 555-5143 by 8:30 p.m.

E. NUMBER PRACTICE

NOTE: Focus on accuracy rather than speed as you practice the number drills.

16 Adding 10 and 20 and 30 and 40 and 70 totals 170.
17 On July 25, 1994, 130 girls ran in a 4-mile race.
18 Al selected Nos. 16, 17, 18, 19, and 20 to study.
19 The test took 10 hours and 8 minutes to complete.
20 Alice took 14 men and 23 women to the 128 events.

21 Did the 33 men drive 567 miles on Route 23 or 27?
22 On 10/29/94, she keyed lines 16-47 in 35 minutes.
23 In 1993 there were 2,934 people in the 239 camps.
24 The 18 shows were sold out by 8:37 on October 18.
25 On April 29-30 we will be open from 7:45 to 9:30.

F. PROGRESSIVE PRACTICE: NUMBERS

Turn to the Progressive Practice: Numbers routine at the back of the book. Take six 30-second timed writings.

Follow the directions at the top of the page for beginning the activity.

LESSON 8 New Keys

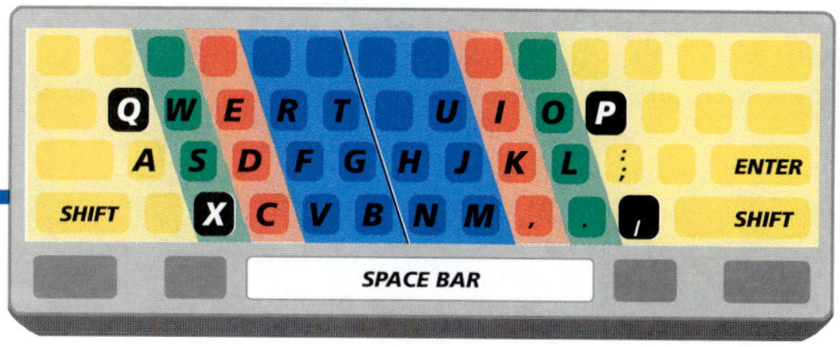

Margins: 1 inch • Spacing: Single • Drills: 2 times

Goals:
To control the P, Q, slash, and X keys; to key 17 wam/1'/3e.

A. WARMUP

1 Jack asked Morgan if Charlie came home.
2 Keith went to lunch with Vic and Baker.

NEW KEYS

B. THE P KEY

Use the Sem finger.

3 ;;; ;p; ;p; p;p ;;; ;p; ;p; p;p ;;; ;p;
4 pan sap rap pad pen sip lip dip pat rip
5 page pale stop trip pace peep palm park
6 Pat Page kept him in step with Pauline.

C. THE Q KEY

Use the A finger.

7 aaa aqa aqa qaq aaa aqa aqa qaq aaa aqa
8 quip aqua quick quiet equip quack quite
9 quell quark quotas quarts quills quests
10 The quiet quints quilted an aqua quilt.

D. THE / KEY

Use the Sem finger.

Do not space before or after a slash.

11 ;;; ;/; ;/; /;/ ;;; ;/; ;/; /;/ ;;; ;/;
12 his/her him/her he/she either/or ad/add
13 do/due/dew hale/hail fir/fur heard/herd
14 Ask him/her if he/she and/or Al can go.

E. THE X KEY

Use the S finger.

15 sss sxs sxs xsx sss sxs sxs xsx sss sxs
16 vex box tax nix mix wax lux lax hex fox
17 axle next taxi flux text flax flex apex
18 Max coaxed six men to fix a sixth taxi.

H. Take a 1-minute timed writing on the first paragraph to establish your base speed. Then take successive 1-minute timed writings on the other paragraphs. As soon as you equal or exceed your base speed on one paragraph, advance to the next one.

H. SUSTAINED PRACTICE: NUMBERS

```
     In the past quarter, we have added the names 10
of 178 clients to our database.  This gives us an 20
exciting total of 249 clients in this first year. 30

     Of the 249 clients, 92 were being handled by 10
Charles Thompson; 84 were controlled by Charlotte 20
Baines; and 73 were being serviced by Gail Banks. 30

     We got 24 clients in July from 108 contacts; 10
August brought us 20 clients from 138 contacts; a 20
record of 34 clients was gained during September. 30

     We were able to get 249 clients in our first 10
year; our aim is 470, 733, and 880 clients in the 20
next three years--or 2,332 clients in four years. 30
| 1 | 2 | 3 | 4 | 5 | 6 | 7 | 8 | 9 | 10
```

I. Spacing: double. Take two 2-minute timed writings. Compute your speed and count errors.

Goal: 21 wam/2'/5e

I. 2-MINUTE TIMED WRITING

```
     We can expect quite a few changes in our job 10
market in the next few years.  There will be jobs 20
that have new skills due to the many uses of the  30
computer.  The labor market will increase in its  40
size, too.                                        42
| 1 | 2 | 3 | 4 | 5 | 6 | 7 | 8 | 9 | 10
```

14 LESSON Number Keys

Margins: 1 inch • Tab: 0.5 inch • Spacing: Single • Drills: 2 times

Goals:
To control the 5 and 6 keys; to key 22 wam/2'/5e.

A. WARMUP

```
     Liza Quigley moved to 4397 South Main Street 10
on July 20.  She expected Frank would spend a few 20
extra hours helping her move 18 chairs and books. 30
| 1 | 2 | 3 | 4 | 5 | 6 | 7 | 8 | 9 | 10
```

SKILLBUILDING

F. PHRASES

19 and it is | she can do | will he come | he is
20 she said so | who left them | can she drive
21 after all | he voted | just wait to | ask her
22 some needed it | for the firm | did he seem

G. TECHNIQUE PRACTICE: SHIFT KEY

23 Ada, Idaho; Sitka, Alaska; Eaton, Ohio;
24 Mr. and Mrs. Lee; Miss Sabin; Mr. Neal;
25 Mr. Don King; Ms. Sue Bell; Ames, Iowa;
26 Dr. Jo Smith; Mr. Ault; Mrs. Dean Bell;

H. Take two 1-minute timed writings. Compute your speed and count errors.

Goal: 17 wam/1′/3e

H. 1-MINUTE TIMED WRITING

27 George planned that Lu should have five 8
28 boxed lunches. Quint was to pack seven 16
29 mugs. 17

| 1 | 2 | 3 | 4 | 5 | 6 | 7 | 8

LESSON 9 New Keys

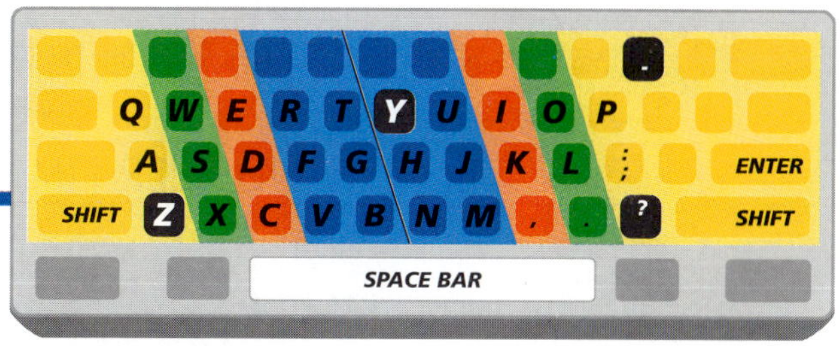

Margins: 1 inch • Spacing: Single • Drills: 2 times

Goals:
To control the hyphen, Z, Y, and ? keys; to key 18 wam/1′/3e.

A. WARMUP

1 I have quit the marketing job in Idaho.
2 Alice packed two boxes of silver disks.

NEW KEYS

B. THE - KEY

Use the Sem finger.

Do not space before or after a hyphen.

Keep the J finger in home position.

3 ;;; ;p; ;-; ;-; -;- ;;; ;-; -;- ;;; ;-;
4 one-sixth one-fifth one-third self-made
5 tie-in ha-ha show-off has-been ice-cold
6 Mr. Ward-Hughes is a well-to-do patron.

C. THE 9 KEY

Use the L finger.

8 lo9l lo9l l99l l99l l9l9 l9l9 9 99 999 9,999 9:99
9 99 lads 99 lights 99 labs 99 legs 99 lips 99 logs
10 Their 99 cans of No. 99 were sold to 99 managers.
11 He had 29 pens, 39 pads, 93 pencils, and 9 clips.

D. THE 1 KEY

Use the A finger.

12 aq1a aq1a a11a a11a a1a1 a1a1 1 11 111 1,111 1:11
13 11 adds 11 arts 11 aims 11 axes 11 aces 11 arenas
14 Sam left here at 1:11; Sue at 11:11; Don at 9:11.
15 Eric moved from 1992 Main Street to 1994 in 1991.

E. THE 0 KEY

Use the Sem finger.

16 ;p0; ;p0; ;00; ;00; ;0;0 ;0;0 0 00 000 0,000 0:00
17 10 pads 10 pegs 10 pits 10 pins 10 pens 100 parks
18 You will get 220 when you add 30, 40, 70, and 80.
19 The 20 men met at 2:02 with 10 agents in Room 20.

SKILLBUILDING

F. NUMBER PRACTICE

20 Jill bought 44 tickets for the 7:30 or 8:30 show.
21 When you add 44, 30, 40, 80, and 90, you get 284.
22 Maxine called from 829-7430 or 829-7431 for Mary.
23 Sally had 12 cats, 20 dogs, and 30 birds at home.

24 Items 37, 38, 39, and 40 were sent on October 18.
25 Did Flight 1478 leave from Gate 19 at 2:30 today?
26 Sue went from 380 29th Street to 471 27th Street.
27 He sold 43 tires, 28 air filters, and 139 wipers.

G. Indent and key each sentence on a separate line.

G. TECHNIQUE PRACTICE: ENTER AND TAB KEYS

28 Casey left. Susan asked for Tom. Where is John?
29 How fast do you key? Is Maxine faster? I drive.
30 She lived at 1991 Main Street. He sold old cars.
31 Do you have the software? If not you, who could?

Elbow Control. Keep your elbows in close, hanging loosely by your sides. Do not let elbows swing out. Keep your shoulders relaxed, fingers curved, and wrists level.

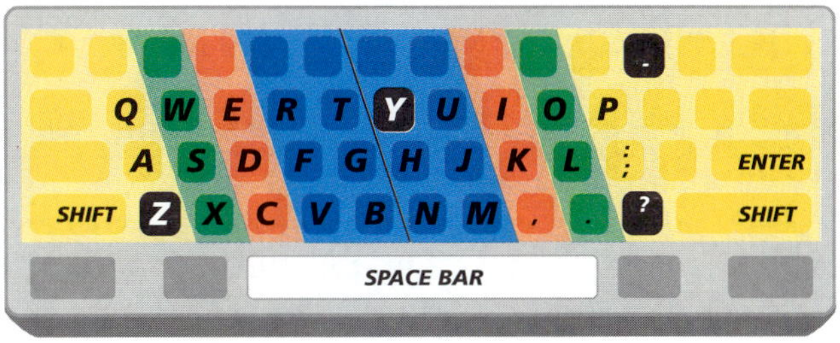

C. THE Z KEY

Use the A finger.

Keep the F finger at home as you reach to Z.

7 aaa aza aza zaz aaa aza aza zaz aaa aza
8 zoo zap zig zip fez daze buzz jazz fizz
9 zing gaze zoom zone zinc quiz zest doze
10 The size of the prized pizza amazed us.

D. THE Y KEY

Use the J finger.

11 jjj jyj jyj yjy jjj jyj jyj yjy jjj jyj
12 ray say way may you joy yam yet yes eye
13 yarn year yawn yard holy fray eyed duty
14 Lucy, Nancy, and Peggy may try to stay.

E. THE ? KEY

The question mark is the shift of the slash.

Use the Sem finger.

Space twice after a question mark at the end of a sentence.

15 ;;; ;/? ;/? ?;? ;;; ;/? ;/? ?;? ;;; ;?;
16 Can Ken go? If not him, who? Can Joe?
17 Is that you? Can it be? Who will see?
18 Did he ask? Can they go? Why not her?

SKILLBUILDING

F. TECHNIQUE PRACTICE: HYPHEN

Hyphens are used:
1. To show that a word is divided (line 19).
2. To make a dash (two hyphens with no space before or after, see lines 20 and 23).
3. To join words in a compound (lines 21, 22, and 24).

19 Can Larry go to the next tennis tourna-
20 ment? I am positive he--like you--will
21 find it a first-class sports event. If
22 he can go, I will get first-rate seats.
23 Zane--like Ellen--liked to write texts.
24 Tony took Liza to a drive-in for lunch.

G. PHRASES

25 and the | for the | car is able | can they go
26 did they fly | ask her | for him | they still
27 of what | with us | ought to be | can he send
28 has been able | they need it | he will call

E. Key each sentence on a separate line.

E. TECHNIQUE PRACTICE: ENTER KEY

```
26 Can he go?  If so, what?  I am lost.  Joe is ill.
27 Did he key the memo?  Tina is going.  Susan lost.
28 Max will drive.  Xenia is in Ohio.  He is taller.
29 Nate is fine; Ty is not.  Who won?  Where is Nan?
30 No, he cannot go.  Is he here?  Where is Roberta?
```

F. Space without pausing.

F. TECHNIQUE PRACTICE: SPACE BAR

```
31 a b c d e f g h i j k l m n o p q r s t u v w x y
32 to an is of we no it in as go by me be or but for
33 Do you go to Ada or Ida for work every day or so?
34 I am sure he can go with you if he has some time.
35 He is to be at the car by the time you get there.
```

G. Spacing: Double
Take two 2-minute timed writings. Compute your speed and count errors.

Goal: 20 wam/2′/5e

G. 2-MINUTE TIMED WRITING

```
36      Skills in expressing our thoughts are needed 10
37 more than ever.  One who can write and speak well 20
38 quite often does well on the job.  You really can 30
39 learn these amazing skills if you will take time. 40
   | 1 | 2 | 3 | 4 | 5 | 6 | 7 | 8 | 9 | 10
```

13 LESSON Number Keys

Margins: 1 inch • Tab: 0.5 inch • Spacing: Single • Drills: 2 times

Goals:
To control the 2, 9, 1, and 0 keys; to key 21 wam/2′/5e.

A. WARMUP

```
1      Quincy Loven took the 3:34 jet to Chicago to 10
2 attend an 8:37 meeting tomorrow.  He expects Fran 20
3 Ladda will have a short buzz session before 7:34. 30
  | 1 | 2 | 3 | 4 | 5 | 6 | 7 | 8 | 9 | 10
```

NEW KEYS

B. THE 2 KEY

Use the S finger.

```
4 sw2s sw2s s22s s22s s2s2 s2s2 2 22 222 2,222 2:22
5 22 subs 22 suns 22 seas 22 sons 22 sets 22 sports
6 The 22 seats sold at 2:22 to 22 coeds in Room 22.
7 He added Items 22, 23, 24, 27, and 28 on Order 2.
```

H. Space once after a semicolon and comma, twice after a period and question mark at the end of a sentence, twice after a colon.

H. PUNCTUATION PRACTICE

29 John sings; Paul writes. Is she there?
30 Can Morgan drive? I will drive; hurry.
31 Pat, Janice, and May left. I will fly.

I. Take two 1-minute timed writings. Compute your speed and count errors.

Goal: 18 wam/1′/3e

I. 1-MINUTE TIMED WRITING

32 Zelig judged six keying contests that a 8
33 local firm held in Piqua. Vic Bass was 16
34 a winner. 18

| 1 | 2 | 3 | 4 | 5 | 6 | 7 | 8

LESSON 10 Review

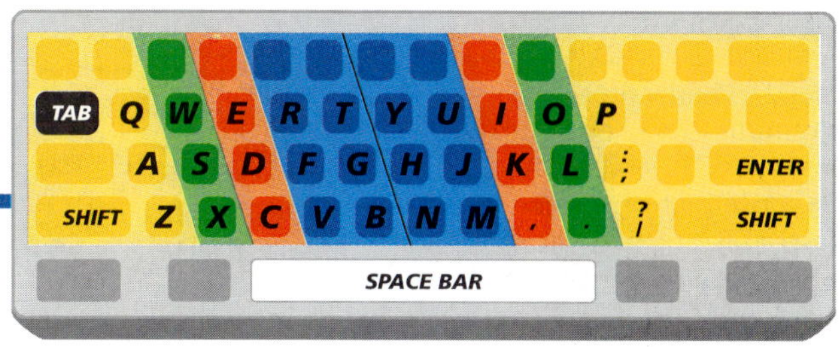

Margins: 1 inch • Spacing: Single • Drills: 2 times

Goals:
To strengthen controls; to format paragraph copy; to key 19 wam/1′/3e.

A. WARMUP

1 Gwen Dunne expects too much from a job.
2 Keith had a very quiet, lazy afternoon.

FORMATTING

The word counts in this book credit you with 1 word (5 strokes) for each paragraph indention in a timed writing. Press the tab key after the timing starts.

B. PARAGRAPH INDENT

When paragraphs are double spaced, the first line of each paragraph should be indented 0.5 inches or 5 spaces (the default setting). Use the tab key to indent. Reach to the tab key with the A finger.

When paragraphs are single spaced, leave 1 blank line between them. The first line may be either indented 0.5 inches or blocked at the left margin. (See illustrations below.)

```
     I would like to visit you

next month.  What plans do you

have during June?

     We could go to Avon for a

trip down the river.  We had a

good time last year.
```

Double-spaced, indented.

```
     I would like to visit you
next month.  What plans do you
have during June?

     We could go to Avon for a
trip down the river.  We had a
good time last year.

     Can you let me know how a
trip like this sounds?  A raft
is a lot of fun, as you know.
```

Single-spaced, indented.

```
I would like to visit you next
month.  What plans do you have
during June?

We could go to Avon for a trip
down the river.  We had a good
time last year.

Can you let me know how a trip
like this sounds?  A raft is a
lot of fun, as you know.
```

Single-spaced, blocked.

LESSON 12 Review

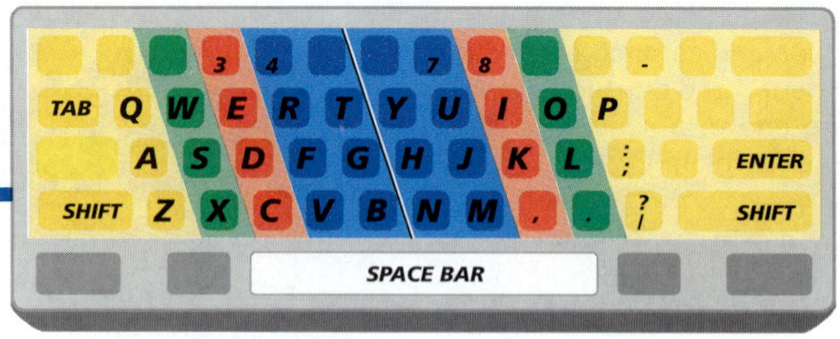

Margins: 1 inch • Tab: 0.5 inch • Spacing: Single • Drills: 2 times

Goal:
To key 20 wam/2′/5e.

A. WARMUP

```
     Alex said 37 men quit unexpectedly.  The men 10
worked in 48 firms.  At least 34 have found a job 20
in 33 firms.  Amazingly, the men like their jobs. 30
| 1 | 2 | 3 | 4 | 5 | 6 | 7 | 8 | 9 | 10
```

SKILLBUILDING

B. SUSTAINED PRACTICE: SYLLABIC INTENSITY

B. Take a 1-minute timed writing on the first paragraph to establish your base speed. Then take successive 1-minute timed writings on the other paragraphs. As soon as you equal or exceed your base speed on one paragraph, advance to the next one.

```
     There is no question that we have entered an 10
age of information.  Many new processes and smart 20
equipment can now provide more data in less time. 30

     The entire telecommunications industry has a 10
very bright future.  With the use of the computer 20
and the phone, much stored data is now available. 30

     The ease with which financial records can be 10
updated and revised is truly phenomenal.  Visit a 20
nearby financial institution for a demonstration. 30

     Inventory control has become simpler with an 10
emphasis on technology.  Optical scanning devices 20
can help businesses with their inventory records. 30
| 1 | 2 | 3 | 4 | 5 | 6 | 7 | 8 | 9 | 10
```

C. ALPHABET PRACTICE

```
Packing jam for the dozen boxes was quite lively.
Fay quickly jumped over the two dozen huge boxes.
We vexed Jack by quietly helping a dozen farmers.
The quick lynx from the zoo just waved a big paw.
Lazy brown dogs do not jump over the quick foxes.
```

D. NUMBER PRACTICE

```
Mary was to read pages 37, 48, 74, and 83 to Zoe.
He invited 43 boys and 48 girls to the 7:34 show.
The 8:37 bus did not come to our stop until 8:44.
Purchase Order 43 listed Items 34, 77, 83, and 8.
Flight 374 will be departing Gate 37 at 8:48 p.m.
```

WP

REVEAL CODES
Alt-F3 or F11

C. WORDPERFECT: REVEAL CODES

When you issue a command, WordPerfect sometimes inserts a hidden code into the document. For example, pressing Enter at the end of a line inserts a hard return code [Hrt]. Use Reveal Codes (Alt-F3 or F11) to view these codes. Reveal Codes splits the screen. The top portion shows text as you keyed it. The bottom portion shows the same text with the codes. To delete a code, position the cursor to the right of the code and press Backspace or position the cursor on the code and press Delete.

To return to the normal screen, press Alt-F3 or F11 again.

WP

LINE SPACING
Sh-F8, 1, 6, *No.*, F7, F7

D. WORDPERFECT: LINE SPACING

Line Spacing sets the amount of space between keyed lines. Single spacing (1) leaves no blank lines; double spacing (2) leaves 1 blank line; triple spacing (3) leaves 2 blank lines, and so forth.

To change line spacing at any point in a document, position the cursor where you wish the new spacing to begin. Enter the appropriate commands (Sh-F8, 1, 6). The default setting is "1" for single spacing. Key "2" for double spacing and so on. All text after the line-spacing code will reflect the new spacing. Line spacing can be changed as often as you wish within a document.

SKILLBUILDING

E. Spacing: double; tab: default. Take a 1-minute timed writing on each paragraph, or key lines 3–8 once. Compute your speed and count errors. Use the tab key to indent the first line of each paragraph.

E. SHORT PARAGRAPHS

3 You can now use your keying skills 8
4 to do many jobs. Quite a few will have 16
5 to be printed. 19
6 It will amaze you to find how easy 8
7 and exact keying is used to rough out a 16
8 good thought. 19

| 1 | 2 | 3 | 4 | 5 | 6 | 7 | 8

F. Spacing: double; tab: default. Key each sentence on a separate line. Tab to indent each line.

Technique hint: Keep your eyes on the copy as you make the reach to the tab key.

F. TECHNIQUE PRACTICE: ENTER AND TAB KEYS

9 Edna asked Quincy to order some stamps.
10 Joseph left for New York at noon today.
11 Mary was amazed to find Robert at home.
12 When is Mary or Lucy to be interviewed?
13 Oscar ordered some pizza for the class.
14 The manager was explicit in directions.
15 Kyle was on time for the short meeting.
16 Who left their worksheets on the table?

G. Take a 1-minute timed writing on the first paragraph to establish your base speed. Then take successive 1-minute timed writings on the other paragraphs. As soon as you equal or exceed your base speed on one paragraph, advance to the next one.

G. SUSTAINED PRACTICE: NUMBERS

24 In the past 34 months, we constructed stores 10
25 in 38 states. We hope to build 47 stores in some 20
26 of the 48 states in which we are currently found. 30

27 Of the 37 stores built, many will have 73 to 10
28 84 employees. In 33 stores, most of the managers 20
29 supervise 34 to 48 employees in all of the units. 30

30 In Ohio, 38 stores serve 43 counties. In 37 10
31 stores, we have over 483 varieties of products to 20
32 sell. All 38 stores sell the Bates 877 products. 30

33 The top 447 stores meet the needs of 874,374 10
34 people in 38 cities in 34 states. Our 43 leading 20
35 stores are found in 33 major cities in Louisiana. 30

| 1 | 2 | 3 | 4 | 5 | 6 | 7 | 8 | 9 | 10

H. Keep other fingers at home as you reach to the shift keys.

H. TECHNIQUE PRACTICE: SHIFT KEY

36 Joe Sal Ann Yuk Sue Pat Jae Tab Fay Vera Rosa Tao
37 Dick Fern Juan Mike Andre Fidel Pedro Chong Alice
38 Karen Ojars Marta Scott Carlos Maria Julie Caesar
39 Al Ken Bob Ray Joan Marge Mary Ted Bill Jerry Mel

I. Keep other fingers and elbow still as you reach to the hyphen.

I. PUNCTUATION PRACTICE

40 Jan Brooks-Smith was a go-between for the author.
41 The off-the-record comment led to a free-for-all.
42 Louis was a jack-of-all-trades as a clerk-typist.
43 Ask Barbara--who is in Central Data--to find out.
44 Joanne is too old-fashioned to be that outspoken.

J. PROGRESSIVE PRACTICE: ALPHABET

Turn to the Progressive Practice: Alphabet routine at the back of the book. Take six 30-second timed writings. Follow the directions at the top of the page for beginning the activity.

K. Spacing: Double
Take two 2-minute timed writings. Compute your speed and count errors.

Goal: 19 wam/2'/5e

K. 2-MINUTE TIMED WRITING

45 If you are seeking a job, do you possess the 10
46 expected skills? Quite often just a list of them 20
47 will let you size up those which you already have 30
48 or may be acquired in your new position. 38

| 1 | 2 | 3 | 4 | 5 | 6 | 7 | 8 | 9 | 10

Reset the line spacing to 1.

G. Key each line twice.

Keep fingers curved and wrists low but not resting on the keyboard as you practice these lines.

G. ALPHABET REVIEW

17 Alma Adams asked Alda to fly to Alaska.
18 Both Bill and Barbara liked basketball.
19 Can Cass accept a classic car in Clare?
20 David did dine in the diner in Drayton.
21 Earl says Elmer edited the entire text.
22 Four fables focused on the five friars.
23 Gina gave a bag of green grapes to Gil.
24 Hal hoped Seth had helped haughty Hugh.
25 Irene liked to pickle pickles in brine.
26 Jody Judd joined a junior jogging team.
27 Keith kept a kayak for a trip to Koyuk.
28 Lance played a razzle-dazzle ball game.
29 Martha made more money on many markups.
30 Nan knew ten men in a main dining room.
31 Opal Olah opened four boxes of oranges.
32 Pat paid to park the plane on the ramp.
33 Quincy quickly quit his quarterly quiz.
34 Robin read rare books in their library.
35 Sal signed, sealed, and sent the lease.
36 Todd caught trout in the little stream.
37 Uncle Marty urged Julie to go to Utica.
38 Viva Vista vetoed the five voice votes.
39 Walt waited while Wilma went to Weston.
40 Xu mixed extra extract exactly as told.
41 Yes, your young sister played a cymbal.
42 Zesty zebras zigzagged in the Ohio zoo.

H. Take two 1-minute timed writings. Compute your speed and count errors.

Goal: 19 wam/1′/3e

H. 1-MINUTE TIMED WRITING

43 Zoe expected a quiet morning to do 8
44 her work. Joy was to bring five of the 16
45 ruled tablets. 19

| 1 | 2 | 3 | 4 | 5 | 6 | 7 | 8

LESSON 11 Number Keys

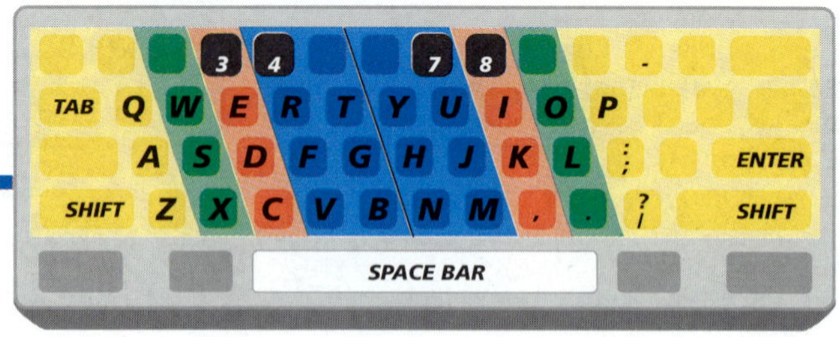

Margins: 1 inch • Tab: 0.5 inch • Spacing: Single • Drills: 2 times

Goals:
To control the 4, 7, 3, and 8 keys; to key 19 wam/2′/5e.

Key the paragraph twice from now on.

A. WARMUP

1 Robert Vaughn wrote a good article in one of
2 our new magazines. He quotes Paul Jones, William
3 Paley, and Xenia May. Read it--you will like it.

| 1 | 2 | 3 | 4 | 5 | 6 | 7 | 8 | 9 | 10

NEW KEYS

B. THE 4 KEY

Use the F finger.

Do not space after a colon used with figures to express time.

4 fr4f fr4f f44f f44f f4f4 f4f4 4 44 444 4,444 4:44
5 44 fins 44 fish 44 feet 44 figs 44 fans 44 flakes
6 The 44 boys had 44 tickets for the games at 4:44.
7 Fred Lyons had read 44 articles and 44 magazines.

C. THE 7 KEY

Use the J finger.

8 ju7j ju7j j77j j77j j7j7 j7j7 7 77 777 7,777 7:77
9 77 jigs 77 jobs 77 jugs 77 jets 77 jars 77 jewels
10 The 77 men bought items 77 and 777 for their job.
11 Joe had 47 books and 77 tablets for a 7:47 class.

D. THE 3 KEY

Use the D finger.

12 de3d de3d d33d d33d d3d3 d3d3 3 33 333 3,333 3:33
13 33 doze 33 died 33 dine 33 days 33 dogs 33 drains
14 The 33 vans moved 73 cases in less than 33 hours.
15 If Charles adds 43, 44, and 347, he will get 434.

E. THE 8 KEY

Use the K finger.

16 ki8k ki8k k88k k88k k8k8 k8k8 8 88 888 8,888 8:88
17 88 inks 88 inns 88 keys 88 kits 88 kids 88 knives
18 Bus 38 left at 3:38 and arrived here at 8:37 p.m.
19 Kenny called Joe at 8:38 at 883-7878 or 484-3878.

SKILLBUILDING

F. NUMBER PRACTICE: 4, 7, 3, AND 8

20 The 47 tickets were for the April 3 show at 8:48.
21 Mary was to read pages 33, 47, 84, and 87 to him.
22 Kate planted 43 tulips, 38 mums, and 87 petunias.
23 Only 387 of the 473 coeds could register at 4:38.

Ten-Key Numeric Keypad

Margins: 1 inch • Spacing: Single • Drills: 2 times

Some computer keyboards contain a separate numeric keypad located to the right of the alpha-numeric keyboard. The ten-key numeric keypad is especially useful for keying large quantities of numbers. The arrangement of the ten-key pad allows for more rapid keying of numbers than is possible using the top row of the alpha-numeric keyboard.

To enter numbers from the ten-key pad, it is necessary to activate the NUM LOCK (NUMERIC LOCK) key. Check to be sure it has been activated (usually indicated by a small light).

On the ten-key pad, 4, 5, and 6 are the home keys. To operate the ten-key pad, place your J, K, and L fingers on the 4, 5, and 6 keys, respectively.

The J finger operates the 1, 4, and 7 keys; the K finger operates the 2, 5, and 8 keys; the L finger operates the 3, 6, 9, and keys; and the thumb operates the 0 key.

Use the Enter key to move the cursor down one line at a time when entering a column of numbers. On most ten-key pads, the Sem finger operates the Enter Key.

Since different computers have different configurations for their ten-key pads, take a moment now to study the arrangement of the keys on your machine.

NEW KEYS

A. THE 4, 5, AND 6 KEYS

Use J, K, and L fingers.

Keep your eyes on the copy.

Press Enter after keying the final digit of each number.

Activity 1

444	455	464
555	466	646
666	544	456
445	566	465
446	644	546
554	655	564
556	454	645
664	545	654
665	565	465
456	656	546

Activity 2

444	555	666
445	554	664
446	556	665
455	544	644
466	566	655
456	546	645
454	545	646
465	564	654
464	565	656
444	555	666

SUPPLEMENTARY TIMED WRITING

Spacing: Double

More and more people are retiring at a younger age as 12
new retirement programs are being offered by business firms 24
and by the government. A good number of the people who 35
retire early may even be starting in a new career or a new 47
job. This is happening at a time when the life expectancy 59
for adults has been quickly rising in the past few years. 70

With the increase in life expectancy and the early 82
retirement plans, it can be seen that adults must be sure 93
to plan carefully for their retirement years. If planning 105
is not done, many people who are in good health could find 117
themselves at this point in their lives with plenty of free 129
time and not much to do. As one ages, it is important to 140
look at the activities that one enjoys and to strengthen 152
one's interest in those things. At the same time, it is 163
important to find new interests and hobbies so that the 174
time in retirement will be enjoyed to its fullest. It 185
should be noted that the financial part of retirement must 197
also be planned in a careful way. One should be sure to 209
check all investments. 213

Of course, some retirees enjoy visiting with family 225
and friends. Others plan to travel as much as they can to 236
many parts of the country or of the world. Then one can 248
find some retirees who pursue a hobby with great zeal. 259
Whatever one wants to do, the most critical factor is that 271
planning must be done with care prior to the date one sets 283
for retirement. In this way, one can be sure to have a 294
retirement that brings success. 300

| 1 | 2 | 3 | 4 | 5 | 6 | 7 | 8 | 9 | 10 | 11 | 12

Use J, K, and L fingers.

Keep your eyes on the copy.

Press Enter after keying the final digit of each number.

B. THE 1, 2, AND 3 KEYS

Activity 1

414	525	636
141	252	363
411	522	633
144	255	366
441	552	663
114	225	336
444	555	666
414	525	636
525	636	414
636	414	525

Activity 2

414	525	636
415	524	634
416	526	635
144	255	366
155	244	355
166	266	344
145	254	364
146	256	365
541	452	463
641	652	563

C. PRACTICE

456	546	645	564	654	123	213	312	231	321
144	145	146	255	254	256	366	365	364	153
441	451	461	552	542	562	663	653	643	624
412	413	414	415	416	412	423	434	445	456
521	523	524	525	526	512	523	534	545	556

Use J, K, and L fingers.

Keep your eyes on the copy.

Press Enter after keying the final digit of each number.

D. THE 7, 8, AND 9 KEYS

Activity 1

474	585	696
747	858	969
477	588	699
744	855	966
447	558	669
774	885	996
444	555	666
417	528	639
528	639	417
639	417	520

Activity 2

417	527	637
418	528	638
419	529	639
147	257	367
148	258	368
149	259	369
744	854	964
745	855	965
746	856	966
747	858	969

SUPPLEMENTARY TIMED WRITING

Spacing: Double

The value of team play and of team effort has been a 12
topic of great interest to many different people. There 24
are experts who look at the actions of people in a variety 36
of research studies in order to find out the impact of a 47
unified effort on how much the group is able to achieve. 59
The results are always the same. When a group of people 70
tries to meet a shared goal, it is quite likely that more 82
will be gained. This is true in many environments--office, 93
plant, home, school, or church. It is especially true when 105
one looks at the success of athletic teams. 113

Many business firms have now begun quality circles in 125
their offices and plants. The goal of these circles is to 137
encourage small groups of workers to meet on a periodic 148
basis to find out if any of the procedures or steps that 160
they follow in the jobs they do can be improved. The small 172
groups give each person in the unit a stake in the way the 184
unit functions as a whole. A quality circle recognizes the 195
benefits that can come from a team effort. 205

The concept of team effort is most evident when it 217
comes to athletic events. Each time that a study is made 229
of a championship team in any sport or event, many comments 241
can be made about the team play and the team spirit that 252
were observed. This point is often discussed after a big 264
game by sportswriters and the many fans of a team. A lot 275
of experts, in fact, would back the notion that team effort 286
is more important than the talents of any single player on 298
any one team. 300

| 1 | 2 | 3 | 4 | 5 | 6 | 7 | 8 | 9 | 10 | 11 | 12

Use the right thumb.

Keep your eyes on the copy.

Press Enter after keying the final digit of each number.

E. THE 0 KEY

Activity 1

400	500	600
401	510	690
402	520	580
403	530	470
404	540	630
405	550	520
406	560	410
407	570	407
408	580	508
409	590	609

Activity 2

700	800	900
701	801	901
702	802	902
703	803	903
104	804	904
105	205	305
106	206	306
107	207	307
108	208	308
109	209	309

F. PRACTICE

751	962	873	503	321	734	520	731	113	791
263	701	228	673	339	491	301	552	677	319
207	553	910	442	406	662	123	456	789	654
540	498	664	205	764	880	969	121	494	757
919	228	337	486	785	513	487	980	225	428

Use L finger.

Keep your eyes on the copy.

Press Enter after keying the final digit of each number.

G. THE . KEY

Activity 1

456	010	.98
123	020	.63
000	030	.40
.01	2.1	.78
.99	0.6	.80
.50	2.4	.50
.78	0.5	.30
.47	6.2	.12
.08	3.6	.90
.09	6.6	.34

Activity 2

4.8	3.3	4.7
6.0	6.3	6.2
9.0	.73	5.0
9.1	.40	9.1
8.0	.30	4.0
7.0	.12	0.2
4.0	.50	0.8
1.0	.03	3.6
5.7	.09	0.3
1.0	.05	7.5

SUPPLEMENTARY TIMED WRITING

Spacing: Double

Since early settlers first came to this land, our 11
people have always had a strong interest in the actions of 23
our government. When you speak of our national, state, or 35
local government, you can be sure that a lively debate will 47
start. This is most true when election time comes and the 58
candidates speak to the issues. Media reports of debates 70
and of election issues tend to be quite broad and can serve 82
as a gauge of what the voters seem to want. 91

Of course, economic issues are bound to start a major 103
debate on the part of those who pay taxes. Raising taxes 114
or changing the tax laws will often start a debate. One 126
other topic that causes much debate deals with our defense 137
plans. Many candidates have used the issue to form their 149
own base for a national election. If you look at the near 161
past, you can see that issues on defense will always be a 172
major concern. 175

In addition to the economic and defense issues, you 187
will be amazed at how rapidly a lively debate can commence 199
over social issues. For instance, crime, education, and 210
privacy are topics that have been of special concern in 221
recent years. There has also been a good deal of debate 233
over the environment, as well as many questions about our 244
welfare system. A lot of our people have a deep interest 251
in the actions of our judicial bodies and the way in which 268
they respond to the social issues that face our nation. It 280
is easy to see that issues under debate by government are 291
sure to be of concern in years to come. 300

| 1 | 2 | 3 | 4 | 5 | 6 | 7 | 8 | 9 | 10 | 11 | 12

Diagnostic Practice: Alphabet

The Diagnostic Practice: Alphabet program is designed to diagnose and then correct your keystroking errors. You may use this program at any time after completing Lesson 9.

Directions

1. Key the Pretest/Posttest passage once, proofread it, and identify errors.
2. Note your results—the number of errors you made on each key and your total number of errors. For example, if you keyed *rhe* for *the,* that would count as 1 error on the letter *t.*
3. For any letter on which you made 2 or more errors, select the corresponding drill lines and key them twice. If you made only 1 error, key the drill once.
4. If you made no errors on the Pretest/Posttest passage, turn to the practice on troublesome pairs on page SB-3 and key each line once. This section provides intensive practice on those pairs of keys commonly confused.
5. Finally, rekey the Pretest/Posttest, and compare your performance with your Pretest.

PRETEST/POSTTEST

```
     Jacob and Zeke Koufax quietly enjoyed jazz music on my
new jukebox.  My six or seven pieces of exquisite equipment
helped both create lovely music by Richard Wagner; I picked
five very quaint waltzes from Gregg Ward's jazz recordings.
```

PRACTICE: INDIVIDUAL REACHES

```
aa Isaac badge carry dared eager faced gains habit dials AA
aa jaunt kayak label mamma Nancy oasis paint Qatar rapid AA
aa safer taken guard vague waves exact yacht Zaire Aaron AA

bb about ebbed ebony rugby fiber elbow amber unbar oboes BB
bb arbor cubic oxbow maybe abate abbot debit libel album BB
bb embed obeys urban tubes Sybil above lobby webby bribe BB

cc acted occur recap icing ulcer emcee uncle ocean force CC
cc scale itchy bucks excel Joyce acute yucca decal micro CC
cc mulch McCoy incur octet birch scrub latch couch cycle CC

dd admit daddy edict Magda ideal older index oddly order DD
dd outdo udder crowd Floyd adapt added Edith Idaho folds DD
dd under modem sword misdo fudge rowdy Lydia adept buddy DD

ee aegis beach cents dense eerie fence germs hence piece EE
ee jewel keyed leads media nerve poems penny reach seize EE
ee teach guest verse Wendy Xerox years zesty aerie begin EE
```

SUPPLEMENTARY TIMED WRITING

Spacing: Double

Many facts and figures are gathered in the first year 12
of each new decade in our nation. These facts and figures 23
are checked by experts in order that some of the new trends 35
and changes facing our country can be noted. For instance, 47
the data that was most recently gathered has given us a lot 59
of insight into the new world of work that is becoming more 71
and more evident today. 76

In the early history of our country, most of the labor 88
market was made up of people who worked on the farm; we 99
were an agrarian nation. We then began to become a country 111
of factory workers. We changed from work on the farm to 123
the mass production of goods in factories. Our workers 134
moved from farm country to the towns and cities. We became 146
a giant industrial nation with the production of cars, 157
steel, coal, and home appliances. We were the leaders of 169
the world in our ability to produce goods, and our standard 181
of living was on a constant rise. 187

The most recent census has shown that a major shift in 199
our work force has taken place. The number of workers who 211
produce goods has continued to shrink, while the number of 223
people who work in the service or information sector has 234
continued to grow. As the median age of our population 246
also continues to rise, there will be even more people who 257
work in this area. Rapid growth in the technology field 269
has surely played a large role in our changing labor market 281
data. As one can see, the changes in labor that have been 293
taking place have been quite dramatic. 300

| 1 | 2 | 3 | 4 | 5 | 6 | 7 | 8 | 9 | 10 | 11 | 12

ff after defer offer jiffy gulfs infer often dwarf cuffs FF
ff awful afoul refer affix edify Wolfe infra aloof scarf FF
ff bluff afoot defer daffy fifty sulfa softy surfs stuff FF

gg again edges egged soggy igloo Elgin angel ogled Marge GG
gg outgo auger pygmy agaze Edgar Egypt buggy light bulge GG
gg singe doggy organ fugle agree hedge began baggy Niger GG

hh ahead abhor chili Nehru ghost Elihu khaki Lhasa unhat HH
hh aloha phony myrrh shale Ethan while yahoo choir jehad HH
hh ghoul Khmer Delhi Ohara photo rhino shake think while HH

ii aired bides cider dices eight fifth vigil highs radii II
ii jiffy kinds lives mired niece oiled piped rigid siren II
ii tired build visit wider exist yield aimed binds cigar II

jj major eject fjord Ouija enjoy Cajun Fijis Benjy bijou JJ
jj banjo jabot jacks jaded jails Japan jaunt jazzy jeans JJ
jj jeeps jeers jelly jerks jibed jiffy jilts joint joker JJ

kk Akron locks vodka peeks mikes sulky links okras larks KK
kk skins Yukon hawks tykes makes socks seeks hiker sulks KK
kk tanks Tokyo jerky pesky nukes gawks maker ducks cheek KK

ll alarm blame clank idled elope flame glows Chloe Iliak LL
ll ankle Lloyd inlet olive plane burly sleet atlas Tulsa LL
ll yowls axles nylon alone blunt claim idler elite flute LL

mm among adman demit pigmy times calms comma unman omits MM
mm armor smell umber axmen lymph gizmo amass admit demon MM
mm dogma imply films mommy omits armed smear bumpy axman MM

nn ankle Abner envoy gnome Johns input knife kilns hymns NN
nn Donna onion apnea Arnes snore undid owned cynic angle NN
nn entry gnash inset knoll nanny onset barns sneer unfit NN

oo aorta bolts coats dolls peony fouls goofs hoped iotas OO
oo jolts kooky loins moral noise poled Roger soaks total OO
oo quote voter would Saxon yo-yo zones bombs colts doles OO

pp apple epoch flips alpha ample input droop puppy sharp PP
pp spunk soups expel typed April Epsom slips helps empty PP
pp unpin optic peppy corps spite upset types apply creep PP

qq Iraqi equal pique roque squad tuque aquae equip toque QQ
qq squab squat squam squaw quail qualm quart queen quell QQ
qq query quest quick quiet quilt quirk quota quote quoth QQ

rr array bring crave drive erode freak grain three irate RR
rr kraft inrun orate Barry tramp urges livre wrote lyric RR
rr Ezars armor broth crown drawl erect freer grade throw RR

SUPPLEMENTARY TIMED WRITING

Spacing: Double

It may come as no surprise that the inability to cope 12
with job-linked stress has been ranked as one of the five 23
biggest threats to American health. More than ten million 35
people in the American work force suffer from many health 47
problems related to stress. In addition, stress has also 58
become the number one work hazard for all kinds of workers. 70

While stress may be a difficult problem for business, 82
not all stress is bad. To the contrary, a stressful work 94
setting can lead to many of the Type A behaviors valued by 106
most of the top firms. However, these traits can quickly 117
turn into a negative. Recent studies show that both men's 129
and women's levels of stress are affected by the way they 141
perceive the events that happen to them, and around them, 152
in both their work and their personal lives. 161

In order for people to relieve some of the stress they 173
find in their lives, they must feel they have some trace of 185
control over what happens to them. The increased business 197
rivalry along with the shrinking of much of the ranks of 208
middle management has forced more people to carry larger 220
work loads. It has also made the competition for a smaller 232
number of top-management jobs a much keener battle. 242

Major employers are expecting to supply a wide range 254
of wellness programs as a way of helping workers deal with 266
stress at work and at home. The types of programs being 277
offered include weight control, stress management, massage, 289
first aid, fitness centers, and blood pressure checks. 300

| 1 | 2 | 3 | 4 | 5 | 6 | 7 | 8 | 9 | 10 | 11 | 12

ss ashen bombs specs binds bares leafs bangs sighs issue SS
ss necks mills teams turns solos stops stirs dress diets SS
ss usury Slavs stows abyss asked stabs cords mares beefs SS

tt attic debts pacts width Ethel often eight itchy alter TT
tt until motto optic earth stops petty couth newts extra TT
tt myths Aztec atone doubt facts veldt ether sight Italy TT

uu audio bumps cured dumps deuce fuels gulps huffy opium UU
uu junta kudos lulls mumps nudge outdo purer ruler super UU
uu tulip revue exult yucca azure auger burns curve duels UU

vv avows event ivory elves envoy overt larva mauve savvy VV
vv avant every rivet Elvis anvil coves curvy divvy avert VV
vv evict given valve ovens serve paves evade wives hover VV

ww awash bwana dwarf brews Gwenn schwa kiwis Elwin unwed WW
ww owner Irwin sweet twins byway awake dwell pewee tower WW
ww Erwin swims twirl awful dwelt Dewey owlet swamp twine WW

xx axiom exile fixed Bronx toxin Sioux Exxon pyxie axman XX
xx exert fixes Leonx oxbow beaux calyx maxim exact sixth XX
xx proxy taxes excel mixed boxer axing Texas sixty epoxy XX

yy maybe bylaw cynic dying eying unify gypsy hypos Benjy YY
yy Tokyo hilly rummy Ronny loyal pygmy diary Syria types YY
yy buyer vying Wyatt epoxy crazy kayak Byram cycle bawdy YY

zz Azure Czech adzes bezel dizzy Franz froze Liszt ritzy ZZ
zz abuzz tizzy hazed czars maize Ginza oozes blitz fuzzy ZZ
zz jazzy mazes mezzo sized woozy Hertz fizzy Hazel Gomez ZZ

PRACTICE: TROUBLESOME PAIRS

A/S Sal said he asked Sara Ash for a sample of the raisins.
B/V Beverly believes Bob behaved very bravely in Beaverton.
C/D Clyde and Dick decided they could decode an old decree.

E/W We wondered whether Andrew waited for Walter and Wendy.
F/G Griffin goofed in figuring their gifted golfer's score.
H/J Joseph joshed with Judith when John jogged to Johnetta.

I/O A novice violinist spoiled Orville Olin's piccolo solo.
K/L Kelly, unlike Blake, liked to walk as quickly as Karla.
M/N Many women managed to move among the mounds of masonry.

O/P A pollster polled a population in Phoenix by telephone.
Q/A Quincy acquired one quality quartz ring at the banquet.
R/T Three skaters traded their tartan trench coats to Bart.

U/Y Buy your supply of gifts during your busy July journey.
X/C The exemptions exceed the expert's wildest expectation.
Z/A Eliza gazed as four lazy zebra zigzagged near a gazebo.

SUPPLEMENTARY TIMED WRITING

Spacing: Double

One of my dear old friends still speaks of the high 11
level of enthusiasm for physical fitness that began more 23
than ten years ago. Millions of people across the country 35
began their own exercise routines, which included a lot of 46
sports activities as well as varied forms of stretching 58
exercises. We were all surprised that such a large number 69
of people began to jog and even to compete in many types of 81
running events. One could find teenagers and people who 93
were more than sixty in the crowd. 100

It is good to see that so many have stayed with the 111
types of routines with which they feel comfortable. Also, 123
hundreds of thousands of others have joined the ranks with 135
each new year. There are now fitness programs set up in 146
the form of teams which compete for points on a weekly or a 158
monthly basis. One is able to earn points based on a scale 170
that seems to be approved by fitness enthusiasts around the 182
country. As one might expect, one can earn more points for 194
running for an hour than for walking. Also, the points 205
that one receives reflect the benefit that is achieved by 217
the body, mostly with respect to strengthening the lungs 228
and the heart. This has been quite a prized gain. 239

In addition to all of the physical benefits one can 250
obtain when sticking with a schedule that provides steady 262
physical activity, an extra side benefit can be found. In 273
all cases, the people who have stayed physically active 285
also have found that their mental state has improved in a 296
very positive way. 300

| 1 | 2 | 3 | 4 | 5 | 6 | 7 | 8 | 9 | 10 | 11 | 12

Diagnostic Practice: Numbers

The Diagnostic Practice: Numbers program is designed to diagnose and then correct your keystroking errors. You may use this program at any time after completing Lesson 14 in the text.

Directions

1. Key the Pretest/Posttest passage once, proofread it, and identify errors.
2. Note your results—the number of errors you made on each key and your total number of errors. For example, if you keyed *24* for *25,* that would count as 1 error on the number *5.*
3. For any number on which you made 2 or more errors, select the corresponding drill lines and key them twice. If you made only 1 error, key the drill once.
4. Make one copy of the drills on page SB-5 that contain all the numbers. (If you made no errors on the Pretest/Posttest passage, key the drills that contain all the numbers, repeat, and then repeat again as you strive to reach new speed levels.)
5. Finally, rekey the Pretest/Posttest, and compare your performance with your Pretest.

PRETEST/POSTTEST

```
     My inventory records dated December 31, 1994, revealed
we had 458 pints, 2,069 quarts, and 4,774 gallons of paint.
We had 2,053 brushes, 568 scrapers, 12,063 wallpaper rolls,
897 knives, 5,692 mixers, 480 ladders, and 371 step stools.
```

PRACTICE: INDIVIDUAL REACHES

```
1 aq aq1 aq1qa 111 ants 101 aunts 131 apples 171 animals a1
They got 11 answers correct for the 11 questions in BE 121.
Those 11 adults loaded the 711 animals between 1 and 2 p.m.
All 111 agreed that 21 of those 31 are worthy of the honor.

2 sw sw2 sw2ws 222 sets 242 steps 226 salads 252 saddles s2
The 272 summer tourists saw the 22 soldiers and 32 sailors.
Your September 2 date was all right for 292 of 322 persons.
The 22 surgeons said 221 of those 225 operations went well.

3 de de3 de3ed 333 dots 303 drops 313 demons 393 dollars d3
Bus 333 departed at 3 p.m. with the 43 dentists and 5 boys.
She left 33 dolls and 73 decoys at 353 West Addison Street.
The 13 doctors helped some of the 33 druggists in Room 336.

4 fr fr4 fr4rf 444 fans 844 farms 444 fishes 644 fiddles f4
My 44 friends bought 84 farms and sold over 144 franchises.
She sold 44 fish and 440 beef dinners for $9.40 per dinner.
The '54 Ford had only 40,434 fairly smooth miles by July 4.
```

SUPPLEMENTARY TIMED WRITING

Spacing: Double

The media has been giving a great deal of attention to 12
the rapid rise in recent years in the number of workers in 24
the health-care profession. For those who do not want to 35
become a nurse or a doctor, there are some other very fine 47
careers that can be pursued to reach the goal of being a 59
part of the health-care field. There are many secretaries 70
with strong skills who can find jobs in a large number of 82
medical settings. The types of work that these people can 94
perform are needed as well by nursing homes, medical supply 106
firms, public health departments, research groups, and 117
medical publishers. Not only must workers in these offices 129
have the skills that are needed by all types of businesses, 141
but they also must be well-versed in medical terminology 152
and in the procedures that are unique to this field. 163

Those who hire office workers for positions in the 174
medical field have a right to expect that those they hire 186
will show great respect for the high ethics one needs in 197
this profession. There has to be a total regard for the 208
private nature of each patient's case. The tasks one might 220
perform often vary from office to office. Some of those 232
who work in this field will have direct involvement with 243
patients who are ill or who may be depressed; one needs to 255
have patience and compassion. There are special programs 267
that prepare people who want careers in the medical field. 279
These can be found at many business schools as well as at 290
a sizable number of other postsecondary schools. 300

| 1 | 2 | 3 | 4 | 5 | 6 | 7 | 8 | 9 | 10 | 11 | 12

5 fr fr5 fr5rf 555 furs 655 foxes 555 flares 455 fingers f5
They now own 155 restaurants, 45 food stores, and 55 farms.
They ordered 45, 55, 65, and 75 yards of that new material.
Flight 855 flew over Farmington at 5:50 p.m. on December 5.

6 jy jy6 jy6yj 666 jets 266 jeeps 666 jewels 866 jaguars j6
Purchase orders numbered 6667 and 6668 were sent yesterday.
Those 66 jazz players played for 46 juveniles in Room 6966.
The 6 judges reviewed the 66 journals on November 16 or 26.

7 ju ju7 ju7uj 777 jays 377 jokes 777 joists 577 juniors j7
The 17 jets carried 977 jocular passengers above 77 cities.
Those 277 jumping beans went to 77 junior scouts on May 17.
The 7 jockeys rode 77 jumpy horses between March 17 and 27.

8 ki ki8 ki8ik 888 keys 488 kites 888 knives 788 kittens k8
My 8 kennels housed 83 dogs, 28 kids, and 88 other animals.
The 18 kind ladies tied 88 knots in the 880 pieces of rope.
The 8 men saw 88 kelp bass, 38 kingfish, and 98 king crabs.

9 lo lo9 lo9ol 999 lads 599 larks 999 ladies 699 leaders 19
All 999 leaves fell from the 9 large oaks at 389 Largemont.
The 99 linemen put 399 large rolls of tape on for 19 games.
Those 99 lawyers put 899 legal-size sheets in the 19 limos.

0 ;p ;p0 ;p0p; 100 pens 900 pages 200 pandas 800 pencils ;0
There were 1,000 people who lived in the 300 private homes.
The 10 party stores are open from 1:00 p.m. until 9:00 p.m.
They edited 500 pages in 1 book and 1,000 pages in 2 books.

All numbers

ala s2s d3d f4f f5f j6j j7j k8k 191 ;0; Add 5 and 9 and 16.
Those 67 jumpsuits were shipped to 238 Birch on October 14.
Invoices numbered 294 and 307 are to be paid by November 5.
Flight 674 is scheduled to leave from Gate 18 at 11:35 a.m.

All numbers

ala s2s d3d f4f f5f j6j j7j k8k 191 ;0; Add 6 and 8 and 29.
That 349-page script called for 18 actors and 20 actresses.
The check for $50 was sent to 705 Garfield Street, not 507.
The 14 researchers asked the 469 Californians 23 questions.

All numbers

ala s2s d3d f4f f5f j6j j7j k8k 191 ;0; Add 3 and 4 and 70.
They built 1,200 houses on the 345-acre site by the canyon.
Her research showed that gold was at 397 in September 1994.
For $868 extra, they bought 27 new books and 62 used books.

All numbers

ala s2s d3d f4f f5f j6j j7j k8k 191 ;0; Add 5 and 7 and 68.
A bank auditor arrived on May 26, 1994, and left on May 30.
The 4 owners open the stores from 9:30 a.m. until 6:00 p.m.
After 1,374 miles on the bus, she must then drive 185 more.

SUPPLEMENTARY TIMED WRITING

Spacing: Double

Most people go through three distinct stages as they 12
progress through their career. Each stage differs from the 24
others in the tasks a person is expected to perform well in 36
that stage, the types of contacts he or she makes, and the 47
manner in which the person perceives his or her role. In 59
the first stage, an employee must work under the guidance 71
of others as an apprentice, helping and learning from one 82
or more mentors. Most of the work in this stage is fairly 94
routine, but it is crucial for the person not to become 105
bogged down in just detail work. He or she is expected to 117
take some first steps and be creative in finding solutions 129
to problems. 131

In the next stage, employees should begin to show that 143
they are people who can really make things happen. They 155
should focus on bringing their skills up to a fairly high 166
level. One way to gain such competence is to cultivate a 178
sphere of expertise. Building a name for competence will 190
greatly increase employees' visibility within the firm, 201
which, in turn, will help them move on to the next stage of 213
their careers. 216

The third stage is called the mentor stage because of 228
the increased effort people make for guiding, influencing, 239
leading, and developing other folks within the firm. At 251
this stage, people are at ease with their qualifications, 262
skills, and talents and are working toward extending their 274
interests within the company. Another key feature is the 286
ability to analyze the direction of the company or some 297
major part of it. 300

| 1 | 2 | 3 | 4 | 5 | 6 | 7 | 8 | 9 | 10 | 11 | 12

Progressive Practice: Alphabet

This skillbuilding routine contains a series of 30-second timed writings that range from 16 wam to 70 wam. The first time you use these timed writings, select a passage that is 2 words a minute higher than your current speed. Take five 30-second timed writings on the passage, trying to complete it within 30 seconds with no errors. When you have achieved your goal, record your results. Then move on to the next passage and repeat the procedure.

16 wam An author is the creator of a document.

18 wam Access means to call up data out of storage.

20 wam A byte represents one character to your computer.

22 wam To store means to insert data in memory for later use.

24 wam Soft copy is text that is displayed on your display screen.

26 wam Memory is the part of a word processor that stores information.

28 wam A menu is a list of choices to guide the operator through a function.

30 wam A sheet feeder is a device that will insert sheets of paper into a printer.

32 wam Boilerplate copy is a reusable passage that is stored until needed in a program.

34 wam Downtime is the length of time that equipment is not usable because of a malfunction.

36 wam To execute means to perform an action specified by an operator or by the computer program.

38 wam Output is the result of a word processing operation. It is in either printed or magnetic form.

40 wam Format refers to the physical features which affect the appearance and arrangement of your document.

42 wam A font is a set of type of one size or style which includes all letters, numbers, and punctuation marks.

56 wam

Going to work has always been a major part of being an adult. Of course, many adolescents also have jobs that can keep them extremely busy. The work one does or the job one holds is a critical factor in determining many other things about the way a person is able to live.

Various work habits are as crucial to one's success as the actual job skills and knowledge that one brings to that job. If one is dependable, organized, accurate, efficient, cooperative, enthusiastic, and understanding, one should be recognized quickly by most supervisors.

58 wam

Being dependable is a desirable trait to have. When a worker says that something will be done by a specific time, it is quite assuring to a manager to know that a dependable worker is assigned to it. Workers who are dependable learn to utilize their time to achieve maximum results.

This trait can also be evident with workers who have a good record for attendance. If a firm is to be productive, it is essential to have workers on the job. Of course, the dependable employee not only is on the job, but also is the worker who can be counted on to be there on time.

60 wam

Organization is another trait that can be described as necessary to exhibiting good work habits. To be organized, a worker should have a sense of being able to plan the work that is to be done and then to work that plan. It is quite common to observe that competent workers are well organized.

If an office worker is organized, requests are handled promptly, correspondence is answered quickly, and projects do not accumulate on the desk. In addition, an organized office worker returns all telephone calls without delay and makes a list of activities to be accomplished on a daily basis.

44 wam Ergonomics is the science of adapting working conditions or equipment to meet most physical needs of workers.

46 wam Home position is the starting position of a document; it is typically the upper left corner of the display screen.

48 wam An electronic typewriter is a word processor which has only limited functions; it may or may not have a visual display.

50 wam An optical scanner is a device that can read text and enter it into a word processor without the need to rekeyboard the data.

52 wam Hardware refers to the physical equipment used, such as the central processing unit, display screen, keyboard, printer, or drive.

54 wam A peripheral device is any piece of equipment that extends the capabilities of a computer system but is not necessary for its operation.

56 wam A split screen displays two or more different images at the same time; it can, for example, display two different pages of a legal document.

58 wam A daisy wheel is a printing element that is made of plastic or metal and is used on different printers. Each character is at the end of a spoke.

60 wam A cursor is a special character, often a blinking box or an underscore, which shows where the next keyed character will appear on the display screen.

62 wam The hot zone is the area before the right margin, typically five to ten characters wide, where words may have to be divided or transferred to another line.

64 wam Turnaround time is the length of time needed for a document to be keyboarded, edited, proofread, corrected if required, printed, and returned to the executive.

66 wam A local area network is a system that uses cable or another means to allow high-speed communication among various kinds of electronic equipment within a small area.

68 wam To search and replace means to direct the word processor to locate a character, word, or group of words wherever it occurs in the document and replace it with newer text.

70 wam Indexing is the ability of a word processor to accumulate a list of words that appear in a document, including the page numbers, and then to print it out in alphabetic order.

50 wam

We all want to work in a pleasant environment where we are surrounded with jovial people who never make a mistake. The realities of the real world tell us, however, that this likely will not happen; the use of corrective action may be required.

For the very reason that this trait is so difficult to cultivate, all of us should strive to improve the manner in which we accept constructive criticism. By recognizing the positive intent of supervisors, each of us will accrue extra benefits.

52 wam

The worker and the firm might be compared in some ways with a child and the family unit. Just as a child at times disagrees with a parent, the worker might question policies of the organization. In both cases, policies must exist for conflict resolution.

One option for a vexed child is to run away from home; an employee may type a letter of resignation. A far better option in both situations is the discussion of differences. The child remains loyal to family, and the employee remains loyal to the company.

54 wam

The person who aspires to a role in management must be equal to the challenge. Individuals who have supervisory responsibilities must make fine judgments as decisions are formed that affect the entire organization. The challenge of managing is trying and lonely.

While other labels are sometimes used to explain basic management functions, the concepts remain the same. The four main functions are involved with planning, organizing, actuating, and controlling of such components as personnel, production, and sales of products.

Progressive Practice: Numbers

This skillbuilding routine contains a series of 30-second timed writings that range from 16 wam to 68 wam. The first time you use these timed writings, select a passage that is 4 to 6 words a minute *lower* than your current alphabetic speed. (The reason for selecting a lower speed goal is that sentences with numbers are more difficult to key.) Take five 30-second timed writings on the passage, trying to complete it within 30 seconds with no errors. When you have achieved your goal, move on to the next passage and repeat the procedure.

16 wam There were now 21 children in Room 211.

18 wam Fewer than 12 of the 121 boxes have arrived.

20 wam Maybe 2 of the 21 applicants met all 12 criteria.

22 wam There were 34 letters addressed to 434 West Cranbrook.

24 wam Jan reported that there were 434 freshmen and 43 transfers.

26 wam The principal assigned 3 of those 4 students to Room 343 at noon.

28 wam Only 1 or 2 of the 34 latest invoices were more than 1 page in length.

30 wam They met 11 of the 12 players who received awards from 3 of the 4 coaches.

32 wam Those 5 vans carried 46 passengers on the first trip and 65 on the next 3 trips.

34 wam We first saw 3 and then 4 beautiful eagles on Route 65 at 5 a.m. on Monday, June 12.

36 wam The 6 companies produced 51 of the 62 records that received awards for 3 of 4 categories.

38 wam The 12 trucks hauled the 87 cows and 65 horses to the farm, which was about 21 miles northeast.

40 wam She moved from 87 Bayview Drive to 657 Cole Street and then 3 blocks south to 412 Gulbranson Avenue.

42 wam Newly employed workers are quite often judged by their skills in informal verbal situations. A simple exchange of greetings when being introduced to a client is an example that illustrates one situation.

A new employee might have a very good idea at a small-group meeting. However, unless that idea can be verbalized to the other members in a clear, concise manner, they won't develop a proper appreciation.

44 wam Many supervisors state that they want their workers to use what they refer to as common sense. Common sense tells a person to answer the phone, to open the mail, and to lock the door at the end of the working day.

It is easy to see that this trait equates with the use of sound judgment. The prize employee should desire to capitalize on each new experience that will help him or her to use better judgment when making decisions.

46 wam Every person should set as a goal the proper balancing of the principal components in one's life. Few people will disagree with the conviction that the family is the most important of the four main ingredients in a human life.

Experts in the career education field are quick to say that family must be joined with leisure time, vocation, and citizenship in order to encompass one's full "career." The right balance results in satisfaction and success.

48 wam As we become an information society, there is an ever-increasing awareness of office costs. Such costs are labor intensive, and those who must justify them are increasingly concerned about workers' use of time management principles.

Researchers in the time management area have developed several techniques for examining office tasks and analyzing routines. The realization that "time is money" is only the beginning and must be followed with an educational program.

42 wam My 7 or 8 buyers ordered 7 dozen in sizes 5 and 6 after the 14 to 32 percent discounts had been granted.

44 wam There were 34 women and 121 men waiting in line at the gate for the 65 to 87 tickets to the Cape Cod concert.

46 wam Steve had listed 5 or 6 items on Purchase Order 241 when he saw that Purchase Requisition 87 contained 3 or 4 more.

48 wam The item numbered 278 will sell for about 90 percent of the value of the 16 items that have a code number shown as 435.

50 wam The manager stated that 98 of the 750 randomly selected new valves had about 264 defects, far in excess of the usual 31 norm.

52 wam Half of the 625 volunteers received about 90 percent of the charity pledges. Approximately 83 of the 147 agencies will get funds.

54 wam Merico hired 94 part-time workers to help the 378 full-time employees during that 62-day period when sales go up by 150 percent or more.

56 wam Kaye only hit 1 for 6 in the first 29 games after an 8-game streak in which she batted 0 for 4. She then hit at a .573 average for 3 games.

58 wam The courier delivered 98 letters during the week to 734 Oak Street and also delivered 52 letters to 610 Pioneer Road as he returned on Route 58.

60 wam Pat said that about 1 of 5 of the 379 swimmers had a chance of being among the top 20. The finest 6 of those 48 divers will receive about 16 awards.

62 wam It rained from 3 to 6 inches, and 18 of the 21 farmers were fearful that 4 to 7 inches more would flood about 950 acres along 3 miles of the new Route 78.

64 wam The 7 sacks weighed 48 pounds, more than the 30 pounds that I had thought. All 24 think the 92-pound bag is at least 6 or 9 or 15 pounds beyond what it weighs.

66 wam They ordered 7 of those 8 options for 54 of the 63 vehicles last month. They now own over 120 dump trucks for use in 9 of the 15 regions in the new 20-county area.

68 wam Andrew was 8 or 9 years old when they moved to 632 Glendale Street from the 1700 block of Horseshoe Lane about 45 miles directly southwest of Boca Raton, Florida 33434.

32 wam

Whichever career path is selected, the degree of pride shown in one's work has to be at a high level. Others will judge you by how well you do your work.

Your self-image is affected by what you believe others think of you as well as by what you think of yourself. The quality of your efforts impacts on both.

34 wam

If a matter is important to a supervisor or to a firm, it should be important to the employee too. The competent person can be relied on to prioritize and complete.

The higher your job-satisfaction level, the greater is the likelihood that you will be pleased with all aspects of your life. Positive attitudes will bring rewards.

36 wam

Whenever people work together, attention must be given to the human relations factor. A quality organization will concern itself with interpersonal skills needed by workers.

Respect, courtesy, and patience are examples of just a few of the words that combine to bring about positive human relationships in the office as well as in other situations.

38 wam

The alarm didn't go off. The road was detoured. The baby-sitter is sick. The car wouldn't start. And for some, the list of excuses goes on. Be thankful that this list is not yours.

You will keep the tardy times to a minimum by planning and anticipating. And you will realize that those who jump the gun by quitting work early at the end of the day have a bad habit.

40 wam

Some people take forever to become acquainted with the office routines. Some must have every task explained along with a list of things to be done. Some go ahead and search for new things to do.

Initiative is a trait that managers look for in people who are promoted while on the job. A prized promotion with a nice pay raise can be the reward for demonstrating that a person has new ideas.

Paced Practice

The Paced Practice skillbuilding routine builds speed and accuracy in short, easy steps, using individualized goals and immediate feedback. You may use this program at any time after completing Lesson 9.

This section contains a series of 2-minute timed writings for speeds ranging from 12 wam to 60 wam. The first time you use these timed writings, select a passage that is 2 wam higher than your current keyboarding speed. Use this two-stage practice pattern to achieve each speed goal—first concentrate on speed, and then work on accuracy.

If you are not using the correlated software, have someone call out each 1/4-minute interval as you key. Strive to be at the appropriate point in the passage marked by a small superior number at each 1/4-minute interval.

SPEED GOAL. Take three 2-minute timed writings on the same passage until you can complete it in 2 minutes without regard to errors.

When you have achieved your speed goal, work on accuracy.

ACCURACY GOAL. To key accurately, you need to slow down—just a bit. Therefore, to reach your accuracy goal, drop back 2 wam to the previous passage. Take three 2-minute timed writings on this passage until you can complete it in 2 minutes with no more than 2 errors.

For example, if you achieved a speed goal of 32 wam, you should then work on an accuracy goal of 30 wam. When you have achieved the 30 wam for accuracy, you would then move up 4 wam (for example, to the 34 wam passage) and work for speed again.

12 wam

What is the[1] meaning of work?[2] Why do most[3] people work?[4]

The concept[1] of work and careers[2] is of interest[3] to you.[4]

14 wam

When doing something[1] that is required,[2] you think[3] of it as working.[4]

When doing something[1] that you[2] want to do, you think[3] of it as fun.[4]

16 wam

We often do not[1] consider the amount[2] of time and effort[3] spent doing a task.[4]

If we did, we would[1] realize that many[2] people work hard[3] even while playing.[4]

18 wam

For example, people[1] sweat, strain, or even[2] suffer from discomfort[3] when playing sports.[4]

People do this for[1] fun. If they were required[2] to do this, they might[3] not be willing.[4]

20 wam

Spending time on a job is work. For most people, work is something they have to do to survive.

Today, work means more than staying alive. People expect different rewards from their jobs.

22 wam

Work can be interesting, and more and more workers are now saying that their work should be interesting.

Sure, there are many boring jobs, and every job always has some less exciting and more routine features.

24 wam

Today there are many different types of jobs which you may choose from which range from the routine to the exotic.

If you begin your planning early, you can work at different types of jobs and learn from the experience of each.

26 wam

Workers tend to identify with their careers, and their careers in a real sense give them a sense of importance and belonging.

People's jobs also help determine how they spend their spare time, who their friends are, and sometimes even where they live.

28 wam

Work can take place in school, in a factory or office, at home, or outside; it can be done for money or experience or even voluntarily.

It should be quite clear that work can be any activity that involves a type of responsibility. The same thing can be said about a job.

30 wam

A career relates to work that is done for pay. But it means more than a particular job; it is the pattern of work done throughout your lifetime.

A career suggests looking ahead, planning, and setting goals and reaching them. The well-planned career becomes a part of the individual's life.